Praise for Paul Ferrini's Books

"The most important book I have read. I study it like a bible!" Elisabeth Kubler-Ross, M.D.

"These words embody tolerance, universality, love and compassion—hallmarks of all Great Teachings. They turn our attention inward to our own divine nature, instead of diverting it outward. Paul Ferrini is a modern-day Kahlil Gibran—poet, mystic, visionary, teller of truth." Larry Dossey, M.D.

"Paul Ferrini leads us skillfully and courageously beyond shame, blame and attachment to our wounds into the depths of self-forgiveness. His work is a must-read for all people who are ready to take responsibility for their own healing." John Bradshaw.

"A breath of fresh air in an often musty and cluttered domain. With sweetness, clarity, and simplicity we are directed to the truth within. I read this book whenever my heart directs, which is often." Pat Rodegast.

"Paul Ferrini's writing is authentic, delightful and wise. It reconnects the reader to the Spirit Within, to that place where even our deepest wounds can be healed." Joan Borysenko, Ph.D.

"I feel that this work comes from a continuous friendship with the deepest part of the Self. I trust its wisdom." Coleman Barks, poet and translator.

"Paul Ferrini's wonderful books show a way to walk lightly with joy on planet earth." Gerald Jampolsky, M.D.

"Paul Ferrini leads us on a gentle journey to our true source of joy and happiness—inside ourselves." Ken Keyes

Book Design by Paul Ferrini
Layout by Aryeh Swisa

ISBN # 1-879159-23-6

Miracle of Love

Reflections of the Christ Mind

Part III

Paul Ferrini

Table of Contents

You have focused so much on how great I am,
you have forgotten your own greatness.
You have neglected the fact that forgiveness cannot
be offered to the world except through you.

Prologue

A teaching lives only to the extent that people understand it and live it. It is like a musical composition. It doesn't come alive until someone performs it.

Performances can be wide ranging in their accuracy and inspiration. Those who are deeply moved by a piece, understand all aspects of it, and have the skills to play it, will give the best performance. They in turn will inspire others to listen and to play.

When I lived, my words and my deeds were congruent. I understood deeply. I spoke simply and clearly. My actions were consistent with my words. That is why people were moved by what I had to say.

When you understand my teaching and practice it in your daily life, you will be a beacon for others. Through you, my teaching will come alive. Through your life, I will live.

This is my second coming. I will not come again in a physical body. I will come through your heart/mind and your life as you attune to me, just as I have always done.

There was a time when I had twelve apostles. Now I have thousands.

Every time a person turns to me in complete surrender, he becomes my instrument. Through his hands and heart I work to spread love in the world.

Every time a person releases her grievances and offers forgiveness to others and to herself, I stand at her side. I am the one who holds her in my arms and comforts her. I am the one who bows with her at the feet of the invisible God.

My disciples practice love and forgiveness every day. They are not perfect in their practice. But they are sincere. They make mistakes, come to recognize those mistakes, and endeavor to learn from them.

My disciples are wise, but they do not parade their wisdom. They do not seek to attract attention to themselves, but work to empower others in their thoughts, their speech and their actions.

No church or temple can bring you to me until you are ready. And when you are ready, you do not need another to intercede in your behalf with me. You have only to ask, and I will be there for you.

Unlike many whom you know, I am not fickle. I do not come and go away from you. Even when you reject me and call me names, I do not stop loving you or cease to see your greatness. For I have learned from my Father and Mother how to love without ceasing, and how to give without expecting anything in return.

When you are ready, you too will learn. If you are turning these pages, that time may be now. I welcome you, brother or sister. As you open to the truth herein, that truth will open in you.

Jesus

I
My Teaching

Words and concepts
will not open your heart.
Only love can open your heart.

I am a Simple Man

I am writing this to set the record straight. It is nearly 2,000 years since my birth and my teaching, which was once like a raging stream, has shrunk to barely a trickle of water. You have rationalized me and put me in my place: an exalted place perhaps, but a distant one. You have placed me above you where I will not challenge you. By making me a deity, an *only* son of God, you excuse yourself from having to live up to my example. Yet my example is the heart of my teaching. If you do not try to emulate me, what is the meaning of your belief in me?

Mine is not an intellectual teaching. It is a practical one. "Love your neighbor" is not an abstract, intricate concept. It is a simple, compelling idea that invites you to practice. I did not invite you to an evening of discourse and argument. I did not ask you to profess or debate the scriptures. I asked you to do what you find so difficult to do: to go beyond your limited concept of self. Any of the practices I gave to you will keep you busy for a lifetime. Although they are simple to understand, their challenge lies in the practice.

If I died for your sins, then there is nothing left for

you to do. Why then not ascend to heaven on the strength of your belief in me?

I will tell you why. Because, in spite of your belief, you are not happy. You are not at peace. That is because you have placed me outside of yourself. You have put me above you, where I cannot touch you.

Take me down from the pedestal, my brother or sister, and place me at your side, where I belong. I am your absolute, unconditional equal. What I have done, you too will do, and more. You will not be saved by my thoughts and actions, but by your own. Except you become the Christ, peace will not come to the world. If you would see me as king, then king must you yourself be.

Do not put this distance between us, for I am no different from you. Whatever you are — a beggar or thief, a holy man or a king — that I am too. There is no pedestal I have not been lifted upon, nor any gutter I have not lain in. It is only because I have touched the heart of both joy and pain that I can walk through the doors of compassion.

I was born to a simple woman in a barn. She was no more a virgin than your mother was. You make her special for the same reason that you make me special: to put distance between us, to claim that what I did you cannot do.

If my life has any meaning to you at all, you must know that I do not claim a special place. Neither Mary nor I is more spiritual than you. We are like you in every way. Your pain is our pain. Your joy is our joy. If this were not true, we could not come to teach.

Do not hold us at arm's length. Embrace us as your equal. Mary could have been your mother. I could have been your son.

Love Is Our Teacher

Whoever you are, whatever your life looks like, know that our understanding and compassion reach to you. It is impossible for you to be in a place that we have not experienced, a place to which the hand of love and compassion does not reach.

We have entered every darkness the soul can fathom. But the light of truth lives even in the darkest of places. There is no such thing as total absence of light. Darkness cannot exist except in reference to the light. No matter how great your pain, it is measured in the degree to which you feel the love's absence or loss. All darkness is a journey toward light. All pain is a journey toward love without conditions.

That is why you are here: to enter the darkness you perceive in yourself and others and to find the light which lives there. Once you find the light, no matter how tiny or insignificant it seems, your life will never be the same. A light bearer never questions the light s/he carries. And so s/he can offer it to others patiently and without fear.

You who seek converts in my name, know that your actions betray your own fear. For love is gentle and kind. It gives without thought of return. It does not ask people to change, but accepts them as they are. No one can minister in my name and withhold love and acceptance. S/he who offers love with conditions, no matter what those conditions are, takes my name in vain.

You must recognize your own fallibility, as I was forced to recognize mine. When you make up the rules, love is constricted or denied. No one is as great as Love, not you or I. And it is to Love that both of us must bow. Love is and will always be our teacher. Will we be its students and learn what it has to teach us? Or will we insist on writing the syllabus and interpreting the text?

The Jewish Perspective

As you know, I am a Jew. When you are a Jew, you do not stop being a Jew and become a Christian. You remain always a Jew. And if you are a true Jew, then you are always asking questions of God. You are always pushing God to the limits. Every day when a Jew prays, s/he asks God "Why?", knowing that God alone has the answers. It is blasphemous when a Jew thinks that s/he knows, for only God knows. At best we have a glimpse of the mystery.

If you wish to follow my teaching, you must first fulfill the Jewish part of your Judeo-Christian legacy. You must know that God has the answers, not you or I. You must submit to life as it unfolds, knowing that there is a purpose, even if you cannot see it.

As a Jew, your attitude must never be full of pride or the pretension of knowing. You must always say "No matter what I seem to know, God knows more than I. God is mysterious. No matter how hard I try, I cannot fathom the Divine way. At best I can have experiences of grace and glimpses of the divine plan. I am the student. God is the teacher. More than that: God is my teacher. *He maketh me to lie down beside still waters. He restoreth my soul.*" As a Jew, you must have a relationship with God.

And it must be a respectful relationship.

Many Christians think that they have my ear and therefore they do not have to dialogue with God. They think they can have me and dispense with God. But it is not true. Without God, I am nothing. It is precisely because I dwell in respect and rapture at the feet of God that I am able to extend the divine blessing to you.

My friends, especially those of you who call yourself Christians, understand that when it comes to God and Jesus, only one of us is dispensable, and I assure you it is not God. You do not need me to come to God. You need only come to the Divine with boundless love and respect. You need only come with a sincere desire to learn. That is how I approached God and that is how you too must approach the Divine, whether or not you believe in me.

You Christians place far too much emphasis on your belief in me. I say, forget me, and remember your Creator. Then, you will be remembering me by your example, not just by your words. If you know me in your hearts, you know that I am not much for words. Show me what you believe not just through your words, but through your actions.

Deeds Not Words

My whole life is about practice. Anyone who practices being loving returns to the divine home. It does not matter what path s/he takes or what s/he calls it.

No one way is better than another. You will not get home faster if you believe in me than you will if you believe in Krishna or Buddha. The man or woman who loves the most makes the most progress. That is the simple truth.

Religions, sects, dogmas are nothing but obstacles on the journey home. Anyone who thinks he has the one and only truth builds his house on quicksand. It will not take long before he discovers that his pride, narrow-mindedness, and lack of tolerance toward others were the cause of his undoing.

If you are a loving person, does it matter if you are Jewish, or Muslim, or Taoist? That love expresses itself regardless of what you believe. The language of love is not a language of words. You may use words, but love does not depend on the words that you use. A few simple words and a heartfelt gesture are enough to convey your acceptance and celebration of another person.

Words and concepts will not open your heart. Only love can open your heart. When you open to the love that is available to you and extend it freely to others, the words that you need will be given to you. You will not have to struggle to know what to say or to do.

When love is in your heart, the path opens before you. Actions flow spontaneously from you. There is no self-consciousness, ambivalence, or deliberation. For these are not the qualities of love. Love is unconditional and direct. It always finds the beloved, even when she is hiding.

The Shepherd Returns

There is no one who will refuse love when it is offered without conditions. And who will offer it but you, my brother or sister?

Today you will drink deeply from the fountain of my love. Tomorrow you will be the fountain. Tomorrow you will carry the gift you have been given into the world. You are the hands of God bringing comfort and healing. And as you give, so you will receive.

In the past, you have given and received through the lens of your fear. But that time is over. Now you know that your fear can never keep you safe. It just holds you apart from the love you want. It keeps you in exile from those who love you and need your love.

You can remain apart from the community of faith as long as you want. But the love of that community will not leave you, nor will it cease expecting your return. For your gift is needed, my brother or sister. And until you learn to trust that gift and give it, you cannot be happy.

When you are ready to come back, your family will welcome you. The family of faith never rejects anyone, no matter how scared or confused that person may be. For this family is the embodiment of love. It is the living example, the word made flesh as the heart opens to love and mind opens to non-judgment.

Come, my brother and sister. Lay your burdens down. Why hold onto your pain and suffering when love's promise can be fulfilled right here, right now? Why hold onto shame or blame when the breeze of forgiveness blows through the land, lifting hearts burdened by grievances and thoughts of retribution? Lay your burden down, my friend. Can't you see that your worries and fears and all the attachments they uphold will not fit through the doorway of truth?

The time of ambivalence and deliberation is over now. When the door opens, you will walk through it. For that is why you came. And no attachment to the affairs of the world can prevent you from fulfill-ing your spiritual destiny. Like all children, you will return home. And returning, you will go forth as I did and guide others to the source of joy and peace.

When the flock is lost, the shepherd appears. And you, my friend, are no less shepherd than I. In the times that come, many shepherds will be needed. Many witnesses to the power of love and forgive-ness will be asked to stand. Through their example, my teaching will live and flower as it never has before. For when one person is certain of the king-dom and offers a loving hand, others follow easily.

II
My Disciples

There is no one who will refuse love
when it is offered without conditions.
And who will offer it but you,
my brother or sister?
Today you will drink deeply
from the fountain of my love.
Tomorrow you will be the fountain.

If You Would Follow Me

If you want to follow my example, practice my teaching of love and forgiveness. Practice giving and receiving love in all of your affairs...in your family, with your friends, in your community, indeed even with strangers.

Do not let the differences in your beliefs, your culture, or the color of your skin keep you apart from each other. For these things are just the external mantle covering the truth of who you are. If you want to know the truth, you must learn to look beyond appearances. You must learn to look not just with your eyes, but with your heart. When you do that, you will not see an adversary, but a brother, a sister, a friend.

When you look with the heart, you feel your friend's pain and confusion. You feel compassion for the universal experience of suffering, which you both share. From that compassion, love is born.... Not the love that wants to fix or change others, but the love that accepts, affirms, reaches out, befriends and empowers.

Love is the only door to a spiritual life. Without love, there are just dogmas and rigid, fearful beliefs. Without love, there is no compassion or charity.

Those who judge others, preach to them, and seek to redeem them are just projecting their own fear and inadequacy. They use the words of religion as a substitute for the love they are unable to give or receive. Many of those who are most forlorn and cut off from love live in the shadow of the pulpit and mount the steps of judgment every Sunday to spread the message of their own fear. Do not judge them, for they are in their own painful way crying out for love. But do not accept the guilt they would lay at your feet. It is not yours.

Those who live a genuinely spiritual life — regardless of the tradition they follow — are centered in their love for God and their fellow beings. When they meet, they have only good wishes and praises for one another. For them, labels mean nothing. For those who practice their faith, God is the only King of Kings, and men and women, no matter what they believe, are absolute, unconditional equals. All are equally loved and valued by God. There are no outcasts, no heathens.

I have said it before and I will say it again: Religious dogma, self-righteousness, and false pride create division, ostracism, and alienation. They are the tools of judgment, not of love. You cannot follow me and think you know what life means or what God intends.

My disciples learn to look upon all that happens with an open heart and an open mind. They grow increasingly willing to surrender their narrow beliefs and prejudices. They refrain from condemning themselves or others for the mistakes they make, but try to learn from these mistakes so that they will not repeat them.

My disciples grow more respectful and intimate in their relationship with God every day. They learn to let the indwelling God lead the way in their lives. Thinking of me and attending to my example help them do this. But they do not make the mistake of thinking that they must do as I do. For their guidance must come from their own hearts, just as my guidance comes from mine.

Being a Christian is not as easy as you think. It means that you open to the possibility of your own Christhood. You accept your potential to become one with God, to open your heart and your mind to God's love and guidance. It means that you stop finding fault with others and begin to look at your own fears as they arise, taking full responsibility for your thoughts and feelings, instead of projecting them onto others. You become honest with yourself, and gentle with others. Your life is your teaching, and it is lived with loving deeds, not with harsh, unforgiving words.

How many people who profess to be Christians live in this way? And so I ask you "How can you be a Christian and not practice giving and receiving love without conditions?" Better to throw away all your other beliefs and hold to this practice than to study scripture and practice judgment.

The path I have laid out for you is an open one. Anyone who wants to can follow it. No prerequisites are necessary: no baptisms, confessions or communions. Nothing external can prevent you from embracing my teaching.

But this does not mean that you will be ready to walk this path. If you are still holding onto your dogma or creeds, you will not be able to take the first step. If you are convinced that you or anyone else is evil or guilty, you cannot step forth. If you think you already have the answers, you may begin to walk, but you will be on a different path.

My path is open to all, yet few will follow it. Few are willing to give up what they think they know to learn what they know not yet. This is how it was when I first walked the path, and it is how it is today. Many are called, but few answer the call.

That is how it is. Do not despair about it. For if you have chosen to walk the path, it matters not what choice others make. Your happiness is your responsibility.

As you walk with the light in your hands, people will approach you and ask how they too can find the light. And, if you are my disciples, you will say to them: "The light is already within you, my brother or sister. You have but to recognize it." You will not ask them to jump through endless verbal hoops or participate in rituals that mean nothing to them. You will embrace them spontaneously. You will welcome them into your community and there they will feel at home. For there is no one who does not feel at home when s/he is loved and accepted unconditionally.

If you want to enter the path I have set out for you, you must take me off the pedestal. You must take Mary off the pedestal. Every one of you is either a Son of God or a Mother of God. If you think otherwise, you have not offered yourself the forgiveness that we offer you.

If you do not see innocence in yourself and others, learn to look with your heart rather than with your eyes. Lest you learn to offer forgiveness to yourself and others, you cannot take your place next to us. And I assure you that place awaits you.

You live in a world where everyone is made guilty. Everyone is made wrong. And most teachings come down on you like a sledge hammer, offering correction at best, condemnation at worst.

My teaching is not like that. I tell you that you are not evil. You are not guilty, no matter what you have done, no matter how many mistakes you have made. I recall you to the truth about yourself. You are a daughter or son of God, no less loved than Mary or me.

Once you accept God's love for you, you will learn from your mistakes. You will no longer want to throw your life away. Forgiveness will lie in the place where evil once seemed to be. And compassion will be offered, where anger and envy once held sway.

Love brings all of us into line. It connects us to our true nature. Our challenge is always a simple one: to open to the love that is there for us.

How do we do this? We do this by refusing to condemn ourselves or our brothers and sisters. We do this by not judging, not complaining, not finding fault. We do this by celebrating our relationships and feeling grateful for the love and nurturing that we have in our lives. We focus on what is there, not on what is not. By finding the good in our own lives, we reinforce it and extend it to others.

As a son or daughter of a loving God, your purpose is to embrace the love that is offered to you and offer it back to others, using whatever skills and talents you have. It matters not what the form of your offering is. What matters is simply that it is given with love.

Who Are My Disciples?

My disciples are those who help people feel connected to the loving God who watches compassionately over all of us. They do not attempt to place me on a pedestal. They do not put obstacles of words or rituals between me and those who would enter the path to truth. They live the love they talk about. They model the teaching.

My disciples know that I did not come to die for their sins, but to recall them to the truth that they are sinless. Experiencing their own sinlessness, they can see the innocence of others, even when others feel unworthy and guilty. My disciples see the light in each soul. They do not focus on the darkness. For they know that darkness is ultimately not real. They overlook apparent evil and injustice by focusing on the indwelling goodness of all beings, for evil is but the absence of something that can never be totally taken away.

By seeing the light in themselves and their brothers

and sisters, my disciples are constantly baptizing. They are always offering communion. Even as people are confessing their sins, my disciples are affirming the Christ within them. Their work is always healing. Like me, they recall people to the truth about themselves.

My disciples do not focus on what is missing or what needs to be corrected. They focus on what is always there and can never be taken away. They focus on what is right and what is good. They do not look for weaknesses and thus they instill strength. They do not look for wounds, and so they help people find their gratitude.

My disciples know that every unkindness that one person does to another is done because there is an apparent lack of love in that person's life. One who attacks others cannot know that s/he is loved.

My disciples teach love by being loving. They teach love by accepting others as they are. In all their actions, they teach others that they are worthy of love. By teaching love, they are filled with peace. And the more peaceful they feel, the more loving they can be.

My disciples know that people often forget the truth about themselves. They become lost in their roles and responsibilities. They take each other for granted. People often feel threatened and build walls of self-protection. They forget to open their hearts. My disciples do not chastise people for forgetting. They simply remind them gently, over and over again, that they are capable of giving and receiving love.

My disciples reinforce the good and the true, and let illusion and falsehood fall away by themselves. They do not berate people for making mistakes, for that would just reinforce the guilt they feel. Instead, they praise people for having the willingness to learn and grow from the mistakes they make.

A Living Example

My teaching is about remembering. It is about becoming conscious of the truth and living it. It is not enough just to know the words. Words are easily forgotten. Words must become practice. And practice must become spontaneous action.

You have focused so much on how great I am, you have forgotten your own greatness. You have neglected the fact that forgiveness cannot be offered to the world except through you. And you cannot offer it, unless you have accepted it for yourself.

When you commune with me, it is not my body

and my blood that you consume, but the spirit of forgiveness, which uplifts your hearts. When you raise the cup, remember your innocence and that of all other beings. That is the lifeblood, the legacy of truth that you must remember and extend.

You think I am special because I was crucified. Yet you are nailed to the cross every day. And when you are not being nailed, you are doing the nailing. There is nothing special about being crucified.

Some of you also believe that I alone was resurrected. Yet you are raised from death by the power of love every time you remember who you are or who your brother is. Every time love is given or received, death is vanquished. For everything dies, except love. Only the love you have given or received lives forever.

You may think that by believing in me you are guaranteed some special place in the afterlife. That is not true, unless your belief in me has inspired you to give love or receive it. If you have not opened to love in your life, your belief in me or in anyone else means very little.

When you remember me, remember what I have empowered you to do in your life, and do not dwell on the "miraculous" things I have done. The power of love will make miracles in your life as wonderful as any attributed to me. For love is the only miracle, not you or me.

We are here to embrace the miracle of love and pass it on to others. Let us not take credit for what love has done or will do. The credit belongs to the one who loved us without conditions long before we knew what love was, or what its absence would mean to us.

We have all strayed from the fold. We have all forgotten the Creator's love. I come to you as a reminder of that love. When you remember my birth into this world, remember my purpose for coming. It is your purpose too.

And your birth into this embodiment is no less holy than mine. Nor will the love you extend to others be any less important than the love that has been offered to you through me. We are all doors to the infinite and eternal and each time your heart opens, spirit makes its appearance in the world.

You are the light of the world. You are the lamb of God come to remind us that we are loved.

The Body and the World

Being in the body is both a privilege and a hardship. Many lessons are learned thanks to the opportunity the body provides. Yet one must remember that everything the body can do for you will one day be undone. The pleasures of food, drink, sex, sleep, entertainment, what will these mean when the body is no longer? To worship the body is as unhelpful as it is to demean it.

The body is a means. It is a vehicle for gathering experience. It has a purpose. I used my body to complete my mission here, just as you must use yours. I experienced physical joy and physical suffering, just as you no doubt have. No one comes into the body who does not explore both ecstasy and pain, love and death.

The body is a vehicle. It is a means for learning. Please do not disrespect or demean it. Please do not make it into a god that you worship. Don't make it more or less important than it is.

When you enjoy and care for your body, it can serve you better. But no body is perfect. All bodies eventually break down. Bodies are not meant to last forever. Nor are they meant to resurrect.

Those who speak of physical ascension or physical

immortality have missed the point entirely. Everything in physical experience is by nature limited. It becomes physical by virtue of the limits that describe it. Take the defining characteristics away, and there can be no physical body. Take the personality away, and there can be no mind, as you know it.

The more definition you have, the more physical you become. That which has a great deal of definition is dense. Ego-orientation is dense. Selfishness and greed are dense. Addiction to substances or states is dense.

Dense means limited and with few options. If you are addicted to alcohol or drugs, how many options do you have? If you are a thief or a murderer, how many options do you have? Dense means your behavior is repetitive, predictable.

All ego states are dense. If you want something to be a certain way and you refuse to compromise or look at things in a different way, you don't have many options. You are taking a limited position. Your beliefs lack insight, flexibility, or compassion. Above all else, your thoughts, feelings and actions are fearful. When you are afraid, you curl up and hold your feet and legs. You contract.

One who acts in a hurtful way to self or others is not evil per se. S/he is fearful, contracted. To atone for hurtful behavior means to adopt a more flexible, open position. And to do this means one must feel safe first. People who feel insecure and unsafe act in rigid, self-protecting ways, even when they are not being threatened.

This is true on all levels. For example, on the level of intellect, conceit or pride comes from insecurity. People who think they know everything generally feel profoundly insecure about their values and beliefs. They are taking a rigid, hostile position.

People aren't born with error. It is something they learn. Take any baby and love it and nurture it and give it wings and it will be a beacon of love. But take the same baby and withhold love from it and refuse to encourage it, and it will sow the seeds of discontent.

There is no original sin. There is no original density. Density is the creation of fear, and fear is learned.

Physical reality seems to be terribly restrictive, but it does not have to be so. I once asked you to be in the world but not of it. I suggested that you be in the body, honor it, use it as a vehicle for spreading love and acceptance, without being attached to it.

I also asked you not to build your house on sand, where every storm takes its devastating toll. Some things are temporary and temporal, and some are eternal. The body is not eternal. The best it can be is a willing servant.

It is futile to be trying always to make the body younger. It is just as futile to seek physical immortality, resurrection, ascension.

My resurrection was not physical. My resurrection was my willingness to go beyond the narrow ideas I found in my life, regardless of the consequences. I accepted torture and death, because I refused to speak anything but the truth that I knew in my heart.

To stand for the truth in the face of opposition is not an easy thing to do. If one values one's body too much, one cannot do it. Only one who values the truth above all else can put himself in harm's way for the sake of what he believes in. Surely, I am not the only one you know who has done that. There are many you know who have risen above their fear to stand up for what they believe in.

But I must tell you that one who does not stand up for truth in a loving way is not serving truth. Means and ends must always be congruent or peace will not be found.

Peace on Earth

Peace is the least dense state you can experience while in a physical body. It has no goal except itself. It has no agenda.

One who is at peace has great flexibility, great patience, great compassion. S/he has no need to try to fix anyone, no need to improve the world. One who is at peace naturally improves the world just by being. S/he breathes peace, talks peace, and walks peace. There is no effort, no attempt to fix.

Nothing in the world is broken. The perception of pain is healed just by seeing it differently. When you look through the eyes of love, there is no situation which cannot be accepted as it is. There is no injustice anywhere apart from the eyes of the beholder. And it is the beholder, in the end, who must let his pain go and see the world differently.

The laws of the world are the laws of the ego. They are based on suspicion and distrust. They seek to control people's behavior. Control is dense. The more we need to control others, the more our own destiny is predictable and controlled.

The laws of Spirit are based on trust and compassion. They speak to the love that lives in every heart and so reinforce it. They see the best in each person and so bring it forth.

This is what I did and what I have asked you to do. Just as I challenged the laws of the world in the name of a higher law, so will you. Because it is not enough to live your life in a state of fear. It is not enough for you to cower in a corner and let other men and women dictate to you.

You must stand up and be counted. But please do so lovingly, compassionately, respectfully. Do it knowing that there is no enemy out there. Each brother or sister, no matter how angry, fearful or distraught, deserves your support and your respect. And how you act means as much, if not more, than what you do or what you say. Angry words or actions do not serve you or anyone else.

When you act in a loving way and speak loving words, the Spirit dwells in you and is awakened in others. Then you are the light of the world, and physical reality is not as dense as it was before. This is the correct meaning of the word ascension.

When love is present, the body and the world are lifted up. They are infused with light, possibility and celebration of goodness. The world you see when Spirit is present in your heart and your life is not the same world that you see when you are preoccupied with your ego needs. The world that you see when you are giving love is not the same world that you see when you are demanding it.

If you want to go beyond the body, learn to use it in a loving way. Think and speak well of yourself and others. Be positive, constructive, helpful. Don't look for problems. Don't dwell on what seems missing. Give love at every opportunity. Bring it to yourself when you are sad. Bring it to others when they are doubting or negative.

Be the presence of love in the world. That is what you are. Everything else is an illusion.

III
The Path of Relationship

*The world you see when you are giving love
is not the same world that you see
when you are demanding it.*

Transforming Negativity

It is important to look at your own negative mind-states so that you can recognize them. Each person must learn to see how s/he creates personal suffering by holding a negative attitude toward the events and circumstances of life. If you don't see how you do this, you will do it unconsciously. And then you won't understand why your life is difficult. You will blame others for your problems: your parents, your spouse, your children, your boss, maybe even God.

I ask you to take responsibility not just for what you do, but for what you think. I ask you to understand the power of your thoughts to create negative emotional states, from which ill-considered actions arise. See how the thought "Nobody loves me" leads to the state of feeling unlovable, disconnected, envious of others who seem to have love in their lives. See how the thought and the subsequent emotional state breed hostile actions, which push others away.

The thought "Nobody loves me" becomes a self-fulfilling prophecy. By thinking this thought, feeling unloved, and acting in a hostile way toward others, you separate yourself from the very love that you want.

Next time the thought "Nobody loves me" comes

into your mind, please be aware of it. If you find yourself becoming depressed, please be aware of it. If you speak or act in a way that separates you from others, please be aware of it. Don't judge yourself or try to change anything. Just bring your awareness to the whole dramatic cycle from thought to action.

Become aware of how your negative mental and emotional states create suffering in your life. See how your negativity becomes a self-fulfilling prophecy. Every time you succeed in separating from others, you substantiate your belief that "Nobody loves me." But the truth is that this experience is your personal creation. It is not true that nobody loves you. The truth is that you don't feel loved.

As you watch your drama unfold, it will be easier for you to take responsibility for it. Then you will begin to tell the truth to yourself. When the thought "Nobody loves me" comes into your mind, you will recognize it and reword it in a more truthful and responsible way: "I see that I am not feeling loved right now."

Instead of trying to make "others" responsible for your not feeling loved, you will be taking responsibility for it. This simple shifting of responsibility for your negative feeling states from "others" to self is the beginning of healing and correction.

When you know that you are not feeling loved, you naturally ask the question "how can I feel loved right now?" What you realize as you explore this important question is that the only way you can "feel" loved is to "think" a loving thought. Loving thoughts lead to the emotional state of feeling loved. And out of this positive emotional state actions arise which connect you to others.

Now, it doesn't matter if this loving thought is about yourself or about someone else. Any loving thought will do. Love is completely unselfish and unselective. Whomever you love will do just fine. When you offer love to another person, you are also offering it to yourself.

When fear and doubt arise in your psyche, you either entertain them or you don't. If you entertain them, you will end up believing that someone else is responsible for your unhappiness and you will feel powerless to change it. If you don't entertain negative thoughts when they arise, you will remind yourself again and again that you are responsible for everything you think, feel, and experience. If you want a different experience, you must choose a different thought. You must substitute a loving thought for a fearful one.

The reason that you are always looking for love

from other people is that you do not realize that love comes only from your own consciousness. It has nothing to do with anyone else. Love comes from your willingness to think loving thoughts, experience loving feelings, and act in trusting, love-inspired ways. If you are willing to do this, your cup will run over. You will constantly have the love that you need, and you will take delight in offering it to others.

The fountainhead of love is within your own heart. Don't look to others to provide the love you need. Don't blame others for withholding their love from you. You don't need their love. You need your love. Love is the only gift you can give yourself. Give it to yourself and the universe resounds with a big "Yes!" Withhold it and the game of hide and seek continues: "looking for love in all the wrong places."

There is only one place you can look for love and find it. No one who has ever looked there has been disappointed.

The Drama of Relationship

In a relationship, it is tempting to believe that the other person holds the key to your happiness. When that person is happy and loving toward you, it is easy to think positively. But when the other person is drained, introspective, expressing negative thoughts and emotions, it is not so easy to stay positive.

How you feel is often determined by how other people treat you. But that is not inevitable. While you can't control how people respond to you, you can choose how you react to their thoughts, feelings and actions.

When people judge you, find fault with you or withhold their love from you, you can realize that they do not feel loved. They are possessed by their doubts and fears. Understand clearly that you are not responsible for how they feel. Don't accept blame. Just be as present and as loving as you can be in that moment. If you can't be present and loving, excuse yourself from the situation. Don't react to the other person's negativity and engage with it. Go into another room. Take a walk by yourself. And work on bringing love and acceptance to yourself.

Keep on loving yourself until you no longer need to look to the other person for positive feedback. When your love for yourself fills you up and comes bubbling over, direct that love toward the other person. Think positive thoughts. Be willing to overlook the other person's negative behavior. Understand that his negativity and self-protectiveness come from his own fear. Feel compassion for the other person's suffering, even if it is self-created. When you see that person, give him a gentle look, a kind word, or a hug. Extend to that person the love you have found inside yourself.

Love does not complain, argue or blame. Love simply embraces the other exactly as s/he is. Love overlooks fear, because fear is not ultimately real. It is a temporary wrinkle in the fabric of life. Wrinkles do not last forever. In the next moment the fabric can be pulled tight and the wrinkle will disappear. Love honors the fabric and knows that it is flexible enough to adjust to new conditions.

No partner is happy all of the time. Don't allow your happiness to be dependent on your partner's happiness. That will just drag both of you down. Tend to your own garden, and offer your partner a rose to smell. Refusing to tend your garden and complaining that your partner never gives you roses will not make either one of you feel better.

When one person is cranky or sad, the other must dig deep inside to find the source of love. When she finds the light within, she must carry it for both people for a while. That way the other person does not forget that the light is there, even if he can't see it in himself.

This does not mean that one person should do all the supporting. Relationships require a give and take. But it does mean that there will be times when each partner will have to rise to the occasion and maintain the connection to Source in the face of the other person's fear and mistrust. That is never an easy thing to do. But it is often necessary in the course of a committed relationship.

Commitment

Your commitment must always be to yourself. When you are committed to yourself, you can make commitments to others. But try to make commitments to others before you have committed to yourself, and you will leave in your wake a trail of heartache and broken relationships.

If you do not do what is necessary to create and maintain your happiness, who will do it? Do you expect your partner to make your decisions and live your life for you? Of course not! You must make your own choices. You are responsible for your own happiness. So go for it! Don't delay! Give yourself permission to move toward your joy and express your gifts. Your willingness to do this is essential to your creative fulfillment. Nobody else can do this for you.

When you have a partner, this responsibility to yourself continues. You cannot give this responsibility to anyone else. It is yours and yours alone. No matter how close you are to your partner, s/he can never be responsible for your successes or failures in this regard.

In a healthy relationship, both people support each other in taking responsibility for their own happiness and creative fulfillment. They offer each other encouragement and positive feedback. And then they let go. They trust the other person to find her own way. They don't judge her goals or interfere in her attempts to realize them.

In a healthy relationship, people are not enmeshed in each other's creative process. Even when they work together, they find a way to support each other's autonomy.

Unless each person has this autonomy and the time and space to grow, he won't command his partner's respect. But autonomy is only one ingredient. Equally important is a shared vision.

Both people must have dreams, values, and aspirations that they hold in common. They must have a vision of a shared life in which they move together as a couple.

When either the autonomy or the shared vision of the partners is weak, the relationship will not prosper. In some relationships, the shared vision is strong, but the autonomy is not sufficient. The couple does not thrive because the individuals are not being challenged to grow. In other relationships, autonomy is strong, but the shared vision and experience is weak. The partners express themselves well as individuals, but do not spend sufficient time together. Their emotional connection is attenuated, and they begin to lose sight of their reason for being together.

Neither of these extremes is helpful. Couples need to work both on expressing themselves as individuals, as well as on strengthening their sense of common purpose. In a healthy partnership, the commitment to self and the commitment to the relationship are equal in depth and intensity.

The Fruits of Partnership

Not everyone is ready to make the commitment to self. Some people enter marriages in order to avoid facing themselves and learning to love and nurture their own lives. Most of these marriages do not last, because there is too much insecurity and neediness on both sides.

In some cases, people can come through such relationships empowered to live their own lives. Here, the relationship becomes a kind of secondary family of origin giving the individual the strength and self-confidence necessary to live on his or her own. Later, when they have lived alone successfully and learned to express their gifts, the two people can enter partnership in a more conscious way, creating a shared purpose with another person.

It is tragic when two people stay together without individuating. It is equally tragic when people stay together without ever creating a shared purpose. One should not have to sacrifice becoming an authentic person in order to create a shared purpose with another. Nor should one have to sacrifice creating a shared reality in order to pursue one's own creative potential. These are not mutually exclusive propositions. They are inclusive and contemporaneous ones. Much of the tension and therefore challenge in relationship lies in the attempt to honor and balance these equally important commitments.

While everyone on the planet must learn to love and accept self, this is only half of our purpose here. The other half is to learn to extend that love and acceptance to another person. We are asked not only to give ourselves permission to move toward our joy in spite of the obstacles that are placed in our way, but also to give our partner permission and support to move toward his or her joy, regardless of its perceived impact on us.

To pretend that any of this is easy for us is absurd. There are lifelong lessons here to which each person must submit in order to find fulfillment and completion.

Relationships offer you a profound spiritual path. Your partner is not only your friend, your lover, and your companion, but also your teacher. S/he reflects back to you all the beauty that lies within you, as well as all the fear, doubt and ambivalence which lies buried deeply within your soul. As you come to accept your partner's apparent imperfections, you begin to integrate your own unacknowledged fears.

There is perhaps no more rapid path to psychological wholeness and spiritual awakening than the path of relationship. It is also one of the most challenging paths.

You must be realistic if you choose to walk this path. While your partnership may occasionally be fun and free of pain — and this is a great goal to aspire to — there may be just as many times when one or both of you is wounded and defensive. Your great accomplishment as a couple is not your ability to navigate around your pain, but your ability to move through your pain together without making the other person responsible for it.

By all means have fun together and celebrate each other's beauty. But do not think you have failed when your fears come up and you begin to see each other as adversaries rather than friends. For, this is the moment when your real work together begins. If you can do this work of inner and outer reconciliation, while still holding onto your joy and mutual reverence, you will build a union which is strong and deep. This is the ground love must be anchored in to grow its brightest flower.

Creating the Love You Want

You cannot force another person to love you the way you want to be loved. Demanding specific expressions of love will only make it more difficult for others to respond to you in good faith.

To be sure, you can ask for what you want. Clear communication is important. But once you have communicated what you want, you must back off and give the other person the time and the space to honor your request to the best of his or her ability.

When you do this, you can observe how deeply your partner hears you and is willing to respond to your preferences. Any effort your partner makes should be positively reinforced. Finding fault with your partner's efforts to please you because they aren't perfect or don't match your pictures of the way things should be will jeopardize his or her responsiveness in the future. In return for your partner's efforts to please you, you can and must relinquish your idealistic pictures and allow yourself to fully receive the gift you have been given.

When you receive your partner's efforts and praise them, you help your partner feel joy and satisfaction in giving to you. That makes him or her want to give more.

Criticizing your partner for not measuring up to your expectations is the fastest way to destroy your relationship. Criticism is not constructive. Gratitude and praise are the building blocks of mutual bliss.

When you don't receive what you asked for, acknowledge what you did receive, and ask again for what you did not receive. Do not ask with anger or resentment. That is a rejection, not a request.

Ask in a kind and respectful way, anticipating that your partner would love to be able to please you, and then give him or her the time and space to respond to you in an authentic way. That way you will have the very best chance of receiving what you want.

Sometimes you can ask in all the right ways, and your partner is still unable to respond to you. When you know you have done your part to communicate your wants and surrender your expectations, you must face the fact that your partner is either unwilling or unable to meet your needs. Usually, when you are honest with your partner, you find that your disappointment and frustration are shared. Your partner doesn't feel that you have responded in good faith to his or her needs and concerns.

When this happens, you have a choice. You can part ways and look for other partners who might be more responsive to each of you. Or you can renew your commitment to each other, and with it your mutual willingness to be loving, accepting and responsive to each other. The latter choice is generally the preferred one, since most relationships can be moved to higher ground when both people stop focusing on what they are not receiving from each other, and instead focus on what they can give to one another.

In the event you and your partner decide to separate, you should do so in a loving way, without holding onto resentments or grievances. You should send each other love and support as often as possible. It is not easy when a relationship ends or changes form, and gentleness on both sides is extremely important if healing is to happen for both people.

When you complete a relationship, consider what you have learned from the other person and be grateful for your experience together. Be cognizant of the issues that separated you and take responsibility for your part in them. When you begin another relationship, be aware of how similar issues arise and see if you can deal with these issues in a more generous and responsible way.

If you are learning from your relationships, you will feel that you are making progress in being a better partner. You will bring increasing honesty and integrity to your relationship and will be better able to create intimacy with your partner as a result.

When the same lessons come up with different partners, bringing familiar discomfort and frustration, you need to consider the probability that something needs to shift inside of you before you can be in a successful relationship with another person. A good therapist may be able to help you look at your relationship patterns, where they come from, and how they can be transformed. When you have gained insight about the ways that you resist intimacy and push love away, you can work consciously to stay open to people who are trying their best to love and accept you. And you can learn to share aspects of yourself that you have always kept hidden.

The beauty of every relationship is that it carries with it great potential for learning. When you are aware of this potential and are willing to delve into it, you can't be disappointed, whatever the outcome of your relationship is. No relationship lasts forever. Each has its natural beginning and end. People come together because they have important things to learn together. When those lessons are learned, they move on to other challenges with other teachers. That is how it is.

The key is not to worry about how long a relationship lasts, but to give it your best energy and attention. Experience as much joy as you can with your partner. Learn as much as you can from the painful times. Do your best to be honest and clear with each other. Stretch your comfort zones a little. Be flexible and constructive. Be the first to yield and to bless. Give without worrying about what you are going to get back. And when you fall down, get back up and laugh at your own stupidity. Your partner — no matter how challenging s/he is — offers you an absolutely stunning opportunity to grow and develop as a compassionate human being.

I could not do a better job than s/he is doing. So do your best to be grateful. Every day, count your blessings. Send love and support to your partner and yourself. Tell each other that you are doing a good job. And urge yourself to keep trusting, keep opening, keep including the other person in your love.

You will never be perfect in your ability to give or receive love. Don't try to be. Just try to be a little more open to give and a little more open to receive than you were before. Remember, you are learning. You are going to make mistakes. You are going to come up short and so is your partner. But accept your mistakes and bless them. Accept your partner's mistakes and send him blessings for his willingness to keep opening to love. That is all either one of you can do.

There is a perfection in your willingness to learn that you can't possibly comprehend, except perhaps if you think of your own children. When you look back at their childhood, you don't dwell on the mistakes they made. You remember the effort they made to reach out, embrace life, and learn from it. You overlook their mistakes and celebrate their indomitable spirit.

If you could look at yourself and your partner with the same compassion, you would put your own errors in perspective. You would celebrate your strengths and forgive your weaknesses. You would see each other in the light of mutual forgiveness and appreciation.

Two people who practice forgiveness on an ongoing basis in their relationship can stay together forever. They may not choose to do this, but there would be nothing that would stop them from doing it if they wanted to. When either one or both of them decide that a change is necessary, they ask for it with love and respect and wait patiently until the other person is ready to accept their request.

There is nothing more healing than the practice of forgiveness in your primary relationships. No other area of your life offers you as many opportunities to understand your wounds and heal them. Your partner is the mid-wife to your birth into your full potential. Thanks to him or her, you learn to surrender the dysfunctional patterns that compromise your happiness. Through the mirror your partner holds up to you, you discover your wholeness and learn to give your gift to the world.

IV
Creativity and Abundance

*Abundance does not mean that you
have a lot of money or material possessions.
It means that you have what you need, use it wisely,
and give what you don't need to others. Your life has
poise, balance, and integrity. You don't have too
little. You don't have too much.*

Creative Energy

All energy is potentially creative. That potential for creation becomes limited as energy expresses itself in form. It is the nature of form to limit and constrict. By limiting its creative potential, form channels and directs energy in specific ways. Form constricts certain energy potentials, enabling other potentials to express themselves in three dimensional reality.

Form chooses. It emphasizes some aspects and de-emphasizes others. It prioritizes. It constructs a picture. Without form, there would be no works of art. Energy would be ubiquitous and therefore invisible, or unmanifest. Manifestation is a commitment of energy to a certain direction or goal. It is the movement from unlimited to limited, from abstract to concrete, to unseen to seen.

All manifest creativity is a dialogue between energy and form. On your level of reality, it is meaningless to talk about energy without also talking about form. It is meaningless to talk about the expression of your creative energy without talking about the choices that you make in your life. What you eat, what you think, how you breathe, and how you speak all determine how energy expresses through your body/mind vehicle. Every choice that you make in your life has an impact on how you give energy or receive it.

You are an animated form, an energy body. Your body/mind consciousness is a temporary container for the universal energy of creation. This energy expresses through you in a unique way, through your genes and chromosomes, as well as through your personality structure. As your mind/body consciousness expands with love, you become more open to giving and receiving the universal energy of creation. Conversely, when you contract in fear, you become less able to give or receive the energy of creation.

It is the nature of energy to expand. It is the nature of form to contract. This is one of the inevitable paradoxes you must live with.

The energy of creation wants to open you up and the structure of your mind and body resists that expansion. The important thing to realize is that all structure belongs to the past, while energy only exists in the moment. It is like water that flows by you as you watch from the bank of a river. It is never the same water you are looking at. In the same manner, the energy inside you is never the same energy that it was five minutes ago. It is always new energy. That is fortunate indeed, because it means that you are never limited to the past. Every adjustment you make in consciousness in the present has an immediate affect on the energy that is able to move through you. As your physical body becomes more healthy and your personality structure becomes more flexible and integrated, you become increasingly able to give and receive energy, physically, emotionally, mentally and spiritually.

You are an ongoing dialogue between energy and form. When you are fearful, you contract on all levels of being. Energy gets trapped in your body/mind and you experience physical tension or pain, emotional upset, and mental anxiety. These symptoms, when not addressed, may lead to bigger ones: physical illness, the break up of a relationship, work or money problems.

On the other hand, when you are feeling loving, energy flows effortlessly through your body/mind. You feel comfortable physically, emotionally strong and flexible, and mentally open and alert. You experience gratitude for what is now in your life and openness to new possibilities.

A fearful attitude toward life leads to defensive, controlling behavior that pushes love and abundance away from you. A loving attitude leads to trusting behavior that honors other people and inspires them to care for you and support you.

Love opens the mind/body consciousness to its maximum energetic potential, enabling others to "feel" the energy of acceptance, gratitude, and kindness flowing directly to them. This opens their hearts and minds to their own potential and empowers them to share their creative gifts with others. This is how abundance is generated in the world.

Ego Blocks to Abundance

The energy of creation is inter-personal and transpersonal. It moves through you to others and through others to you. While this energy supports you in essential ways, there can be no personal ownership of it. No one has a special connection to the energy. As soon as someone claims ownership of it, his or her connection to the energy is disturbed.

When your relationship to each other is one of mutual trust and mutual respect, you create an energetic connection which is supported by the love energy of the universe. That is why I said "When two or more are gathered in my name, there am I."

Your alignment with the energy of creation requires the relinquishment of your ego agenda. Your ego agenda operates from the belief that you can manipulate people and events to obtain the outcome you want. Your ego agenda is selfish and short-sighted. It does not consider the good of others, and therefore it does not consider your good, although you may believe that it does.

When you cheat someone out of something s/he deserves, you lose not only what you thought you would gain, but what you would have gained if you had acted in a less selfish way. Every attempt to gain in a selfish manner eventually leads to loss and defeat, because selfish actions are not supported by the universe.

Those who take advantage of others may have great determination and skill, but they cannot compensate for the loss of their connection to the energy of creation. Others equally determined will join together and, supported by invisible forces, defeat them in the end, for David always defeats Goliath. Not because he is bigger or stronger, but because his intention is clear and he has love in his heart.

While fear might sometimes seem to marshall more forces on its side than love, it can never hold those forces together. Fearful forces are always pulling apart. When the selfish expectations of one group are no longer met, it defects or goes over to the other side.

Love has greater sustaining power than fear,

because it is peaceful and patient. When it does not attract help right away, it does not despair, but finds comfort and faith in the strength and clarity it already has.

I have said that "those who live by the sword will die by the sword." Those who try to take advantage of others will fall victim to their own erroneous actions. That is the nature of the karmic journey. Every time you attempt to injure another, you really only injure yourself. For, everything that you think and do toward others returns in the end to you. Only one who truly forgives and eschews vengeance breaks through the vicious egoic cycle of violence.

If you want to open to abundance in your life you must give up the idea that you can gain through someone else's loss. That is the fearful thinking of the ego mind and it must be recognized and refused if new patterns are to be set into motion in your life.

Fortunately, there is another way, a way that begins when you recognize that your good and that of your brother or sister is one and the same. When you accept your equality with others, then you reconnect to the energy of creation, and that energy supports you.

Because you are supported, you do not toil in vain. Results come spontaneously and on their own timetable. But you are always being asked to relinquish your expectations so that the work can move through you and with you.

While you may have ownership of your area of the work, you never have exclusive ownership of the work as a whole. For the work of creation is essentially collaborative. It cannot be done without the contribution of many people. Your piece needs to fit with other pieces, or the integrity of the whole will be compromised.

The demands of this path are as great as those made by the ego's path of manipulation and struggle. But the rewards of the path of Spirit are far greater, for those who follow this path find true happiness. Because they serve others, love serves them. Because they give without thought of return, the universe brings to them unexpected gifts. Because they live joyfully in the present, the future unfolds gracefully before them. When challenges come, they rise to meet them. When disappointment arises, they look within, and surrender the barriers to love that prevent them from feeling love's presence in their lives.

Four Steps to Freedom from Fear

You believe that your ego knows what is good for you and can bring you what you want. This is not true and has never been true, yet it is a belief you accept every time you adopt one of the ego's strategies. The ego promises you everything you want, but how often does it deliver? If you answer the question honestly, you will have to admit it never delivers what it promises.

All the plans of the ego are motivated by fear. You listen to its voice because you are fearful. If you were not fearful, you would listen to a different voice.

The ego seems to offer you a way out of fear, but how can that which arises out of fear lead you out of fear? It cannot be done. Only that which arises from a place of non-fear can show you a way out of fear.

The key to everything is your recognition of your fear. Once you know that you are fearful, you know that any decision you make while in this state will be counterproductive.

When you are in fear, your only constructive course of action is to recognize your fear, realize that you are incapable of making good decisions, and begin to work on accepting your fear and moving through it.

Here are four simple steps that can help you do this.

First, recognize your fear. Notice the signs that fear is coming up for you: rapid, shallow breathing, pounding heart, nervousness, anxiety, attack thoughts, anger. Be aware of your physical, emotional, and mental state without judging it or trying to change it. Acknowledge it to yourself and, if another person is involved, to the other person.

Second, recognize that the solution the ego offers you is motivated by fear. Understand that your ego will always have a solution to every perceived problem. But, when you listen to that solution, you don't feel any more peaceful. Indeed, you often feel more charged with anger, more victimized, more suspicious of other people and defensive toward them. The ego's solution cannot bring you peace. What it can do is to make you feel more uncomfortable so that you can finally recognize your discomfort.

Third, accept your fear. Get your arms around all of it. Say to yourself "It is okay that I am afraid. Let me be with my fear. Let me tune into why fear is coming up for me right now." Don't be analytical about this. Don't go up into your head. Stay in your emotional body and listen to what's there. You will know when you have listened enough because you will begin to feel more peaceful, even though you don't have a solution to your dilemma.

Fourth, tell yourself "I don't have to decide anything now. I can wait until my fear subsides and insight comes to make any decisions that need to be made."

By doing these four steps, you will bring love and acceptance to yourself. Out of this compassionate place, a non-fearful solution to your dilemma can be found.

But do not put pressure on yourself. Pressure is just more fear coming up. Keep loving yourself and accepting your fear. Be patient and let the answer come from a non-fearful place in your psyche.

Know that the ego does not have a solution for any of your problems. In spite of its perpetual promises to you, it does not know what you need.

No matter how hard it tries, fear cannot bring love. Indeed, the harder it tries, the more it fails. And the more it fails, the harder it tries. There is no end to this downward spiral of laborious and useless effort until fear is accepted as it is and no longer expected to bring a solution. When it's okay to be afraid, fear is off the hook, and so are you.

Hearing God's Answer

Fear is never the enemy, nor is the ego. Everyone has fear. Everyone has an ego. You are not being asked to get rid of your fear, but to be aware of it and accept it. You are not being asked to get rid of your ego, but to acknowledge it compassionately, while seeing clearly that it cannot bring you understanding or peace.

If you want to hear God's answer, you must first hear the ego's answer with compassion. You must say to the scared, hurt, angry one within you "I see that you are afraid and that is okay. I understand that. And I understand what you want to do. I will consider it. But for now I would like to be open to the possibility that there is a better way to look at this than the one we're seeing." Addressing the ego in this loving way calms it down, diminishes its fear, and yet enables it to feel heard. This simple act of speaking to the fearful aspect of self with loving kindness accomplishes a shift in the psyche away from fear.

You cannot be aware of God's presence until you have addressed your fear in a loving way. You set the stage for the Divine with your love and acceptance of all aspects of yourself. You prepare a place in the temple of yourself for God to come.

And God will come. Do this simple practice and you will see. God will come and speak with you. And the voice you hear will bring you peace and understanding. The voice you hear will connect you energetically with the consciousness of love. You will not be the same once you have had communion with God within. For all grievances will fall away. And you will be vibrating with acceptance of your life and everyone in it. You will know its perfection and understand what is being asked of you, even if you cannot put that understanding into words.

When problems arise and fear comes up for you, remember "It's okay to be afraid. It's okay not to know the answer." That is the beginning of your surrender to the Divine within yourself. That which knows cannot take charge until you realize that you don't know and ask for help. As long as you need to be in charge, God can't step in.

And who, my friends, is God but the one in you who knows and understands, the one who loves and accepts you without conditions, under all circumstances, now and for all time? That being is not outside of you, but in your heart of hearts. When you ask sincerely, this is the One who answers. When you knock, this is the One who opens the door.

You cannot come to God when you are in fear and you think you know the answers. First, you must acknowledge your fear and your ignorance. And then you must bless yourself so deeply that even your fear and your ignorance are acceptable. That is the way to the God who loves you without conditions.

And who else would you call upon in your struggle? Would you settle for the conniving voice of the fearful child in you who feels unloved and victimized and would attack or betray others to save his/her own skin? I don't think so!

When you know the choice is between the whining child and the loving Mother, you won't have any difficulty knowing who will comfort you. And when you listen to the voice of the Mother, the fearful child is comforted too.

The Myth of Evil

In truth, mother and child are not separate. They just appear to be. God and the devil are not separate, but appear to be. The child has no authority apart from the mother, nor does the devil have any authority apart from God.

If the devil exists — and he does not exist as a separate, independent being — he exists only as a personification of the collective ego, as a description of a being who is attempting to live in a way contrary to the will of God. If God is all-powerful, which S/he is, because S/he is All That Is, then the devil can stand apart from God only with God's permission. If there is a devil — if there is evil in the world — it can only exist because God allows it to exist.

Why would God allow evil to exist in the world? Why would God allow one of his angels to fall? The answer is "S/he does not." There is no such thing as evil. There is no such thing as the devil.

What you see is not evil, but the perception of evil. You perceive that people are bad. And indeed, their actions seem to confirm this. But they are not bad, although their actions may be unloving and cruel.

If you could change the consciousness of a person so that his actions were loving instead of unloving, would this person still be bad? Of course not! You must allow for the possibility of redemption.

As long as redemption is possible, absolute evil cannot exist. People may act in ways that appear to be "evil," but they only appear to be evil when compared to the actions of other people who appear to be "good." As long as you ask the "evil" one to measure himself in comparison to the "good" one, he will always come up short. He will feel shamed and incapable of changing. You do not empower a guilty man by reinforcing his guilt.

Instead, you tell him that you love him and that he is worthy of love. You tell him that he is really "good," not "evil." You tell him that he has been mistaken about who he is. Others have been mistaken too. Those who abused, neglected, or humiliated him did not know who he was. But you know. And you are telling him now that he is "good" and that you are willing to love him and be his friend.

Can you imagine your society saying this to its hardened criminals: its rapists and murderers? Yet that is what it must do or it will reinforce their guilt and keep the cycle of violence intact.

If you want someone to act in a loving way, you must be willing to love him. Only your love for him will teach him the meaning of love. Empty words and promises will not do.

You, my friend, must love your ego — your angry, abused child — your indwelling devil — your capacity for unloving thoughts and actions — so that this fallen angel, this Christ child hidden in the manger of your heart may be redeemed from false perception and recognized for who S/he is. Until you do this, you cannot experience your wholeness.

You, my friend, must love your enemy — the one on whom you project your own fears and inadequacies — the one you blame for your problems — the devil incarnate in others — so that you may make peace with others and learn to love and embrace yourself.

The inner synergy and the outer healing are inextricably related. As long as you find an enemy within or without, you are fighting the truth about yourself and others. As long as you see evil or devils as something that has reality apart from your own fearful thoughts, you are crucifying yourself and condemning the world.

Such thoughts and beliefs are not helpful. I have told you before and I will tell you again: Be careful whom you condemn. It might be yourself.

In each devil you perceive, there is an angel you must discover, an angel who has fallen and needs your love to ascend. When you offer that love, you will find that you too have risen.

Each person must rise above her fears and prejudices or risk remaining apart from love. For every block to love lies in her own heart and it is there that it must be dissolved.

Don't wait for heaven to come to spread your love around. Do it now. For heaven is here right now. It is in your heart when you open to love. It is in your eyes when you see with acceptance and compassion. It is in your hands when you reach out to help. It is in your mind when you see "good" instead of evil.

How you see the world determines what the world will be for you. As long as you are here, this will be true. So do not seek to change other people or the world around you. But look within your own heart and mind. Hear the criticism, the judgments, the cries for vengeance and you will know where love needs to be brought.

You cannot save your neighbor when your own heart is full of fear. Attend then to your own fear and be not concerned with the fear of others. Until you have listened to your fear and blessed it, you cannot witness to your brother or sister.

Understanding and Compassion

If you want to live with understanding and compassion, you must realize that God is the only authority. Everything is God, including that which tries to live without God. For what tries to live without God is simply a part of God that doesn't accept itself. It is God pretending not to be God.

People who are called "evil" are not separate from God except by their own actions. They feel unloved and act in unloving ways. But God has not stopped loving them. God is not able to stop loving anyone. For God is love, always love, in every moment.

Every sin is but a temporary moment of separation. It cannot be final. Every child who strays from God's love will return, because it is too painful to be separate from the Source of life. When the pain becomes too great, every being turns back. There are no exceptions.

The world is a classroom for redemption. Everyone who comes here tries in one way or another to live apart from God's will. Each person experiences fear and listens to the ego's voice. Some simply realize more quickly than others that they can't find love in separation.

And everyone wants love. Even the ego craves love. It just does not know how to create it.

And so the child who divorces the parent still dreams of the parent's love, but does not know it is the parent's love s/he needs. S/he thinks it is someone else's. And so s/he seeks another to love him or her when no other can or will. Love has been offered and s/he has turned it down.

S/he can turn back and accept the love s/he once turned down. Or s/he can move ahead in stubbornness and pride, seeking a substitute for the love s/he has refused.

That is the choice each of you must make in every moment. Will you turn toward the parent who loves you, or will you turn away in fear? Will you accept or reject God's authority?

God's will for you is not separate from your good, but that is what you must learn. When you are willing to give up your ego's interpretation of the events and circumstances of your life, and let their meaning be revealed to you by the one who understands and wills them to be, you will come to see that everything that happens to you is engineered to open your heart to love's presence. As you open, you move through your fear, and leave it behind you. For you know that fear cannot lead you home. And love cannot mislead you.

The Economy of Love

As you probably know, the body politic will never experience peace and happiness until the people who live in the world experience peace and happiness in their hearts and minds. When they do, the world will look different to them and it will be easier for them to give and receive love and support.

People whose minds and hearts are open experience and extend love, gratitude and abundance as a matter of course. They don't have to do anything special. Being open, what they need comes to them. Being caring and compassionate, they give away what they don't need to others who need it. This is the law of love. It is based on trust and faith.

People who align with the law of love do not have to try to hold onto or protect what they have. For they know that everything they have is merely given to them temporarily. It will stay with them as long as it is needed. And when it is no longer needed, it will go.

People who align with the law of love are always learning to release their attachments so that they can open to the next stage in their growth. They are constantly learning to surrender the ego's terms and conditions to make room for God's will to take root in their lives.

The economy of love is based on surrender. The economy of fear is based on control. The economy of love is rooted in the understanding that there is enough for everyone. The economy of fear is rooted in the belief that there isn't enough to go around.

If you look around you will see both economies at work. The economy of fear seems to be more prevalent than the economy of love, but if you look carefully you will see that the former is losing strength to the latter. That is because the more fearful people become, the more they must learn to rely on love to survive. While conditions seem to be getting worse, in fact they are getting better.

That is the good news. The bad news is that very few of you believe this. Most of you believe the doomsday prophets who say the world is condemned to unimaginable suffering and distress. This belief induces more fear and has the potential to become a self-fulfilling prophecy.

The real struggle before you today is not a struggle between good and evil, but a struggle between your belief in goodness and your belief in evil. Each of you must fight this battle in your own consciousness. And that is where your suffering either deepens or dissolves.

Believing in evil, you contract emotionally, become more defensive, and cut yourself off from the energy of creation. That is the consciousness of scarcity. Believing in good, you expand emotionally, open up to others, and engage with the creative energy of the universe. That is the consciousness of abundance.

Contrary to popular opinion, abundance does not mean that you have a lot of money or material possessions. Abundance means that you have what you need, use it wisely, and give what you don't need to others. Your life has poise, balance, and integrity. You don't have too little. You don't have too much.

On the other hand, scarcity does not mean that you don't have enough money or material possessions. It means that you don't value what you have, don't use it wisely, or don't share it with others. Scarcity may mean that you have too little. It may also mean that you have too much. Your life is out of balance. You want what you don't have, or you have what you don't want or need.

I assure you that you will not increase your happiness by increasing your material possessions. You increase your happiness only by increasing your energy, your self-expression and your love. If that also increases your pocketbook, then so be it. You have more to enjoy and share with others.

The goal in life should not be to accumulate resources that you don't need and cannot possibly use. It should be to earn what you need, enjoy and can share joyfully with others.

The abundant person has no more or less than she can use responsibly and productively. She does not obsess on protecting what she has or in obtaining what she does not have. She is content with what she has, and is open to giving and receiving all the resources that God brings into her life.

V
A Spirituality
of Love and Freedom

Real love does not seek to bind, control, or enslave,
but to liberate, to empower, to set others free
to find their own truth. What church or temple
has this for an agenda? What religious structure
gives its members the freedom to self-actualize
in the name of love?

Beyond the New Age

As dogmatic, hierarchical religious teachings are appropriately rejected, a socio-spiritual gap is created. No longer willing to let outside authorities dictate to them what to believe, people try to find their own way of connecting with God, purpose and meaning in their lives. While this search may be liberating and fruitful for some, it is confusing and emotionally draining for others who may need more social participation and structure in their lives. It is not surprising, perhaps, to see some "recovering new agers" gravitating toward conservative or even fundamentalist churches which offer a stable community where regular fellowship thrives and parents can raise their children in a safe, supportive environment.

The great gift of the new age movement is the freedom it gives individuals to explore many different approaches to spirituality so that they can make their own eclectic and creative synthesis of ideas. It empowers people to ask their own questions and find their own answers. However, those religious structures that emphasize self-exploration and foster diversity often lack the kind of social and emotional cohesiveness found in more homogeneous religious communities which require individuals to conform to the group norms.

For many people, there is a clear choice between freedom and belonging. The more freedom one needs, the less chance one will find a community into which one can fit comfortably. What is empowering for the individual and what strengthens the group culture are by their very nature often at odds.

The weakness of the new age movement is its lack of spiritual depth and emotional congruence. The plethora of self-help books, workshops and seminars synonymous with the phrase "new age" comes in response to a tremendous groundswell of interest in non-dogmatic, non-authoritarian approaches to spirituality. Unfortunately, the fervor of interest in new approaches leads to the development of heavily marketed, superficial tools that promise life changing experiences without delivering them.

The down side of new age consciousness is its "quick fix" mentality, its inference that the answer to all of our problems lies in something outside ourselves. If one tool doesn't work, we can always find another one that does. When there are a thousand approaches to truth, all of them touted by one persuasive person or another, it is hard for people to choose one of them and stick to it. Superficiality and dilettantism tend to be the rule.

As we have seen, not everyone who embarks on a journey of self-empowerment is capable of navigating the spiritual marketplace, sifting and shredding, and finally making an eclectic synthesis of tools and techniques that leads to the experience of inner awakening. While some have used this freedom to explore well, there are more casualties in the age of drive-in spirituality than there are success stories.

Confusion, contradictory beliefs, addiction to books, workshops and new promises of fulfillment lead to a spiritual vacuum or cul de sac. Many new age advocates do not know what they believe or where to turn. Many have not found connection to a loving community. Some have lived selfish, me-centered lives that do not lead to deepening insight or compassion.

The wings that have been given to this generation grow tired now. As many move into the second half of life, there is a need to settle down and grow roots. There is a need for friendship, eternal values, and beliefs that encompass and speak meaningfully to the pain and suffering of the past.

A Free and Loving Community

The great challenge before you today is to learn how to come together to create community based not on dogma or external authority, but on mutual equality and a deep respect for each person's experience. The question is "How do you accept and appreciate the differences between you while maintaining emotional connection and continuity? How do you experience freedom and love at the same time?"

Since most forms of love tend to be conditional, love is offered only when there is perceived agreement. To love someone who disagrees with you is rare. To feel emotionally connected to someone who has a very different set of experiences is unusual.

Real love is unconditional. It does not exclude anyone for any reason. It requires you to see beyond appearances, to see others from an inner conviction that all people carry the divine spark within them.

Real love does not seek to bind, control, or enslave, but to liberate, to empower, to set others free to find their own truth. What church or temple has this for an agenda? What religious structure gives its members the freedom to self-actualize in the name of love?

What church extends love and inclusion to all?

What society reaches out to those who live on the fringes and keeps inviting them back in? What community of human beings is dedicated to seeing beyond its fears and learning to love its enemies?

When I asked for a church, was this not what I asked for? Did I not ask for a community which would recognize the Christ presence in all human beings, a community where no one would be ostracized or cast out? What is salvation, I ask you, if you do not offer it to everyone, regardless of his appearance or beliefs?

Love, my friends, means to give and receive freedom. It means to empower. There are never any guarantees in the act of loving. If you look for agreement or favorable response, you cannot love freely. And if love is not free, it is not love. It is bargaining, negotiation, commerce.

Perhaps you begin to see what a church like the one I called for would do for the world you live in. It would make no one wrong, but encourage each person to find out what is right for him or her. It would trust and support the love and the light that dwells in each human being. It would not foster a world divided into rich and poor, haves and have-nots, but a world in which each person has enough and is not afraid to share what s/he has.

A church and a society founded in my name

would live by the principles I taught and teach. It would extend love and support freely to all. It would make no one wrong, condemn no woman or man, nor ostracize any human being from the community of faith. It would not be defensive, greedy or proud, but open-minded, generous and humble.

These qualities lie within each one of you. You have only to cultivate them. There is not a single one of you who cannot love unconditionally. But you must be encouraged to do so. My church is a church of encouragement. It calls you to realize the highest truth about yourself.

Honoring Father and Mother

If you follow my teachings, you must know that I call upon you to become the embodiment of unconditional love, non-judgment and compassion. I challenge you to accept each person who comes before you as a Child of God, no less perfect than you or I am. I challenge you to give to each the love and freedom Father and Mother God have given you. I call you to love and let go, to nurture and empower, to comfort and inspire.

Love is peaceful, but not static. It is dynamic, but not overwhelming or controlling. It gives the gift you need to receive and receives the gift you need to give. It is both feminine/receptive and masculine/active.

If you want to be a vehicle for love, you must practice both giving and receiving, leading and following, speaking and listening, acting and refraining from action. Love flows to and from you naturally as you accept the polarities of your experience, integrate them, and realize your wholeness.

You are a child of the Father and the Mother, as am I. As a man, you must emulate the father and embrace the qualities of the mother. As a woman, you must emulate the mother and embrace the qualities of the father. Just as God is neither male nor female, but both together, so are you a synthesis of male and female qualities within a particular body/mind vehicle.

Women have an equal place in my teaching. They have always have had that place and they always will have it. Those who have denied women their rightful place in my church will have to answer directly to me.

Gays and lesbians, blacks, Asians, Hispanics, born-agains, fundamentalists, Buddhists, Jews, even lawyers and politicians all have a place in the community of faith. Anyone is welcome. No one should be excluded. And all who participate in the community should have the opportunity to serve in leadership positions.

My teaching has never been exclusive or hierarchical. You have imposed your prejudices and your judgments on the pure truth I have taught. You have taken the house of worship and made it into a prison of fear and guilt. My friends, you are mistaken in your beliefs.

But it is not too late for you to learn from your mistakes. Repent from your unkind actions and words. Make amends to those whom you have injured or judged unfairly. Your mistakes do not condemn you unless you insist on holding onto them. Let them go. You can grow. You can change. You can be wiser than you once were. You can stop being a mouthpiece for fear and become a spokesperson for forgiveness and love.

No ship has ever been refused refuge in the harbor of forgiveness. No matter what you have said or done, I will welcome you home with open arms. All you need do is confess your mistakes and be willing to let them go.

The past cannot condemn you if you are willing to open your heart and mind right here and now. Your willingness to change is the Godforce working within you. And It, not I, will bring you home. I will simply welcome you when you arrive here.

What Is Spirituality?

Spirituality and religion are not necessarily the same thing. Religion is the outer form; spirituality is the inner content. Religion is the husk; spirituality is the seed. Religion is a set of beliefs; spirituality is a continuum of experience.

One can be spiritual and not attend church or temple. One can find one's spirituality in intimate sharing with others, in communion with nature, in being of service. Spiritual experience is simply that which relaxes the mind and uplifts the heart. Meditating, walking in the woods or by the ocean, holding an infant, or looking into a lover's eyes — these are all spiritual experiences. When there is love and acceptance in your heart, your spiritual nature is manifest and you can see the spiritual nature of other people.

To be spiritual is to see yourself and others without judgment, to see not just with the eyes, but with the heart. To be spiritual is to accept and appreciate "what is," instead of seeking "what is not."

A spiritual person sees beauty everywhere, even in suffering. Wherever hearts are touched by the poignancy of life, there is beauty. Whenever people learn their life lessons and let the past fall away, beauty is present. There is beauty in the rain and clouds, and beauty in the sun. There is beauty in aloneness and in intimacy, in laughter and in tears. Wherever we turn, beauty awaits us.

A spiritual person does not focus on what appears to be ugly, cruel, or manipulative. S/he sees all these behaviors as coming from a lack of love. S/he gives love whenever it is asked for, even if it is requested in a fearful or aggressive way. A spiritual person looks upon her own suffering and that of others as a temporary disconnection from the experience of love.

A spiritual person knows that love is the answer to every perceived problem. If life does not unfold the way we want it, we have disconnected from love and acceptance. To reconnect, we need only surrender our expectations and accept what comes into our lives with gratitude.

Spirituality is the consciousness that life is okay the way it is. It doesn't need to be changed or fixed. It just needs to be accepted.

When we make peace with life, we have peace in our lives. It is that simple. We cannot blame anyone else for our unwillingness to make peace.

A spiritual person is peaceful, upbeat, helpful,

encouraging. S/he doesn't complain about the past or look for happiness in the future. S/he doesn't try to fix other people or ask to be fixed. S/he lives in the present moment, filled with gratitude and acceptance.

Everyone is spiritual, but not everyone takes the time to explore spirituality. Many people become lost in the drama of their lives. They spend most of their time dealing with survival issues. They do not take the time to watch the sunset or smell the roses. They are missing out on a great deal of joy and beauty. If they would just stop, take a deep breath and look for a moment, they would realize what they are missing.

A spiritual person is a happy person. S/he refuses to sacrifice that happiness for any reason. S/he does not think thoughts or perform actions that compromise his or her happiness in any moment.

This is the discipline involved in living a spiritual life. There are many people who would draw you into their dramas of suffering and victimhood, but you must learn to say *no* to them. Bless them. Give them the space to have the experience they wish to have. But do not join them in that experience unless you can do so happily.

Do not seek to heal other people or rescue them from their dramas. Your ability to genuinely help them depends on your maintaining your own health and peacefulness. By holding the vibration of your own happiness, you help them see where they can find healing and salvation within themselves.

When you rest in your Self, you see that there are no problems to be fixed. Life just needs to be accepted in a heartfelt way. In that acceptance, peace and happiness are established and all that was obstructing love is dissolved.

Who Needs Religion?

I hate to disappoint you, but the truth is that no one needs religion. You don't need to hold onto the husk. But you do need to break it open and plant the seed.

Whatever your religion is, know that it has dogmas and interpretations that disguise the truth. All religions are heavily burdened by the prejudices and narrow ideas of followers who never opened to truth and beauty in their lives. What you have is a record of their fear, not an invitation to love.

But if you dig deeply enough in the garden of your faith, you will find the voices of truth and beauty that help you to open your heart to love's presence. And that is where you must focus. That is where you will plant the seed of faith that will take root in your life.

There are many beautiful trees that flower in the springtime. One is not better than the other. Each has its special beauty. Seen together, they make an extraordinary garden. So it is with approaches to the divine. Each approach has its own beauty and integrity. It speaks to certain people and not to others. That is the way it should be. One tree is not better than another. One religion is not better than another.

Each religion has attached to it a climate of fear and rigidity that can destroy the tree before its seeds can be carried forth on the wind. This is true in every tradition.

If you belong to a tradition, you must find the seed, separate it from the husk, and see that it is planted in your lifetime. You must find the core teaching that connects you to love and pass that teaching on to your children. That is the only way that a tradition stays healthy. The form should change to better speak to the time and place, but the essence of the teaching must be continually discovered and resurrected.

A barren tree will make no fruit. A religion that does not help its followers connect to love will not prosper.

You do not have to belong to a religion to awaken your spirituality. But it is easier to awaken to the truth and beauty of your life if you belong to a loving community of people. Such a community need not be religious. Many secular groups and communities provide their members with the same emotional support and empowerment that some people find in religious organizations.

You don't have to belong to a community to open your heart to love, but it sure makes it easier if you do. Even if you meet with just two or three other people who are loving and supportive, you will find that it helps you transcend your personal drama and stay open to the purpose and meaning that are unfolding in your life.

That is why I have given you the Affinity Group Process.* It provides you with a very simple way of staying connected to love in your life. It is particularly helpful if you aren't comfortable with religion and don't have a secular support group in your life.

Even if you do belong to a church or support group, you may find that the Affinity Process can help your group or congregation stay connected to love. As groups and organizations grow outwardly, they often forget their purpose and they cease to be nur-

---

The Affinity Group Process is described in the book The Ecstatic Moment *by Paul Ferrini and is available from Heartways Press (see order form in the back of this book).*

turing places for their members. Bringing the Affinity Process into such an environment can reawaken the original inspiration and loving interactions which made the organization popular to begin with.

In the long run though, no organization is going to provide you with ready-made spiritual sustenance. The best a church or temple can do is help you connect to love. Once that connection is made, it is up to you to nurture that love at home with your family, at work, and in all of your interactions with others.

Leading a spiritual life is essential for your fulfillment. But no one can or should tell you what that spiritual life should look like. Your journey is a unique one and you are guided most appropriately by the Spirit within you. As you listen to your inner voice and learn to rely on it, you won't need to depend on your parents, your minister, or other authority figures for guidance. You will establish in your Self. You will become authentic.

That is what it comes to in the end. When the truth has been nurtured within you, it asserts itself clearly in your life. As you become more fully empowered, you may leave your support group, your church or your temple to follow your calling. Then, wherever you go, you give and receive support without hesitation. For when love is awakened within in you, it is given freely to all who need it. And the work of God is extended through your thoughts, your speech and your actions.

In truth, each one of you is a minister of God in training. And you will be called to serve your brothers and sisters when your connection to love is firmly established. When that call comes, you will have no choice but to answer it. For, it is the reason for which you came, the purpose for which you are ideally suited in temperament and ability.

God knows your purpose, even if you do not know it yet. But God lives within you, not outside. And if you would know your purpose, you must ask the divine being within. That is the only one who can guide you home.

Affirmation and Negation

If you want to connect deeply with your spiritual nature you must understand clearly and profoundly what needs to be affirmed and what needs to be denied. On the simplest level, truth is affirmed, and falsehood is denied. Love is affirmed and fear is denied. Essence is affirmed and appearance is denied.

The problem with affirming truth, love and essence is that we often don't know what they are.

How can you affirm the truth if you don't know what it is? How can you affirm love if you are fearful or ambivalent about it? How can you affirm essence if you are always looking for the approval of others?

Often, to approach affirmation genuinely, we must practice negation. If I am confused, I must acknowledge "This confusion is not the truth." If I am ambivalent in my feelings, I must admit "This ambivalence is not love." If I am looking for external reinforcement for how I feel, I must see that "This search for approval is not essence."

By being clear about what truth, love and essence are not, I create the space within me to realize what they are. And so the process continues..."Truth is not prejudice or narrow opinion, love is not expectation or the desire to rescue or fix another, essence is not the search for agreement, approval, or belonging."

In Zen Buddhism, there is a practice of negation that says "Neither this nor that." There is no preference or taking sides. This helps one resist the temptation to find truth in intellectual concepts. Truth is deeper than concepts.

Lao Tzu, the great Chinese sage told us "The way that can be spoken is not the true way." Truth lies in the heart along with essence and love. They cannot be found with the mind or spoken with the lips. They can be embodied and expressed only by one who does not need to be right, loved back or approved of. Real truth, real love, real essence have no opposite, for they do not come from the realm of duality.

To reach real truth, real love, real essence, we must stop attaching to their imitations. If we accept conditional love, we will not experience love without conditions. If we accept any form of dogma, judgment or prejudice as truth, we will not know the pure truth of the heart. If we seek the approval of other men and women and are attached to the way they receive us, we will not tell the truth about ourselves even when it is called for.

We must negate all imitations. Let's be clear that if you are not at peace, you are not experiencing truth or love or essence. For these can be experienced only when you are free of opposition, conflict, ambivalence, attachment, expectation or special interest of any kind. As long as your love is offered with conditions, as long as your truth is offered with judgment of others, as long as your essence is puffed up and attached to self-image, you are offering an imitation.

If you mistake the false for the true, you cannot affirm what is true or deny what is false. That, my friends, is the difficulty of words and concepts. To penetrate to the core, you must go beyond words and concepts.

When you speak of love, please ask yourself "Is my love free of conditions?" When you speak of truth, please ask yourself "Is my truth free of judgment or opinion?" When you speak of essence, ask "Am I attached to the way people perceive or receive me?"

Freedom to be yourself requires more detachment than you think. As long as you want something from anyone, you cannot be yourself. Only when you want nothing in particular from anyone are you free to be yourself and to interact honestly and authentically with others.

I do not say this to discourage you, but to prepare you for the depth and breadth of the journey you are on. To be a self-realized person requires that you disconnect from all expectations and conditions whether they come from you or from another.

Your goal is to accept every person you meet just the way s/he is and to be yourself regardless of how other people receive you or react to you. When you meet someone who revolts you or pushes your buttons, you are not seeing truth or essence in that person. If you feel expansive when people love you and depressed when people dislike you, you are not established in the truth of your own essence.

Love is the most difficult thing in the world and the easiest. It is the most difficult thing because you have so many attachments and expectations that block its flow toward you and from you. It is the easiest because, when you drop those attachments and expectations even for a moment, love comes to you and emanates from you spontaneously and without effort.

VI
Abuse and Forgiveness

You can't see the light in others until you see it in yourself. Once you see it in yourself, there is no one in whom you do not see the light. It does not matter if they see it or not. You know it's there. And it is the light you address when you speak to them.

Fear of Commitment

People who are afraid of love ask for it nonetheless. Yet when it comes to them, they are unable to receive it. They want love to come in a perfect shape and size. And it never comes that way.

Real love comes from essence, not appearance. It is practical and immediate, not ideal or abstract. People who can't look past appearances won't recognize the beloved even when s/he stands before them.

People who are afraid of love are ambivalent about giving and receiving. When you are aloof, they feel safe and desire your presence. But when you come close, they get scared and ask you to back off or go away. This emotionally teasing behavior enables them to be in relationship while avoiding intimacy and commitment.

If you are drawn into such a relationship, you must face the fact that you too may be afraid to receive love. Why else would you choose a partner who cannot give it? More specifically, you may believe that the only way you can receive the love you want is to put up with someone's constant criticism and rejection of you.

Only when you say "Enough!" do you break the magic spell. No matter how good the sex is, no matter how strong the emotional connection, you must learn to stand back and see the game for what it is: "Okay, I finally get it. No matter what I do I will never be acceptable in your eyes. I am not going to play this game anymore."

People who find fault with others are insecure and incapable of trusting their feelings or acting on them. They cannot make a commitment to you because they are not committed to themselves. Lacking a strong connection with their own guidance, they are never sure about what to do. They vacillate from one extreme to the other, always looking outside themselves for reinforcement. If you want stability and commitment, why would you choose to be with someone who is always changing his or her mind?

Your job is not to judge these people, analyze them or try to fix them. Accept them as they are. Send them love. But don't live with them or be their partner. Stop compromising yourself. You deserve love without having to put up with criticism or abuse. Only if you are afraid that no one will love and accept you the way you are would you settle for love with such unfortunate conditions attached to it.

If you are willing to be a victim, you will be sure to attract an abuser. Your lack of faith in yourself attracts another who is similarly insecure. What the other person does to you is just an external version of what you are doing yourself. The message is loud and clear: "Stop beating yourself up."

Don't blame the other person. Take responsibility for the fact that you allowed the criticism to continue and be clear that you are making a different choice. Own the problem and the solution.

Loving and taking care of yourself are essential steps in attracting a relationship that will honor you. Do not accept less than you want and deserve and you will not bring inappropriate relationships into your life.

When you make a mistake, own it. Hear the message that each abuser brings: "Respect and honor yourself."

Whose responsibility is it when you do not honor yourself, when you do not insist on a relationship with a partner who honors you? You see, your suffering is not someone else's fault. It is a direct result of your own beliefs and actions!

If you don't want to play games in your intimate relationships, then look with care when a potential partner comes into your life. Is s/he gentle and forgiving with you, or is s/he critical and controlling? Say yes to the former and no absolutely to the latter.

Unless you can say no to potential partners who are incapable of honoring you, how can you attract a partner who will love and accept you as you are?

You Bring in What You Allow

None of you are victims of someone else's actions toward you. You bring into your life what you allow to come in. If you say "no" to what you *don't* want, you bring in what you *do* want. It is that simple.

The only factor that makes all this complicated is that you don't always know what you want or, if you do, you don't trust it and remain committed to it. When your unconscious desires are different from your conscious goals, what you bring into your life reflects a mixture of both. Your creative capacity functions both consciously and unconsciously. Mind is creative, whether or not it is aware of itself.

If you want to create consciously, you must bring your unconscious desires and fears up for acceptance and inspection. Then, you will understand why your experiences often differ remarkably from what you consciously intend. You can then adjust your goals so that you begin to honor all of you, not just the adult part.

When you understand your desires and fears, you

can make choices that do not violate the more child-ish, vulnerable parts of your psyche. This may mean that your goals become more immediate, short-term and realistic. But this is a positive step, insuring that your long term goals will not be undermined by the scared and wounded aspects of your psyche.

Expecting too much from yourself or from others is as dysfunctional as expecting too little. Wanting a job or relationship you don't have the skills or matu-rity to handle is counterproductive, if not downright traumatic. It is far better to seek out a less challeng-ing job or relationship and do well at it then it is to shoot too high too soon. Small, progressive victories build confidence on all levels of the psyche, inte-grating child and adult perspectives and strengthening trust that will be needed for more dif-ficult challenges that lie ahead.

To create what you want means to get clear about what you really want on all levels of your being. When the spiritual adult and wounded child want different things, manifestation is always mixed. That is why the time you take to integrate and unify the different needs and wants of your psyche is time well-spent. When there is unconflicted desire in the heart and clarity on all levels of consciousness, the creative process flows easily.

If you want to succeed in your relationships with others, take the time to get to know yourself. Then it will be clear when and to whom you must say *no* and when and to whom you must say *yes*. Remember, what comes to you is not always what it seems. The knight in shining armor may be an insecure abuser in disguise and the one offering comfort and support may be a wolf in sheep's clothing.

Always look beyond appearances, for nothing is as it seems to be. When you know what you want and what you need, be patient and wait for it. Many will come to you claiming to be the one you asked for, but only one will be authentic. Usually, it won't be the one who comes with lots of smoke and mirrors. More often than not, it will be the simple unassuming one, the one who doesn't use big words or promise great gifts, but who takes your hand and looks into your eyes without fear.

Equality and Mutual Respect

In order to experience equality with others, you must be willing to treat others with dignity and respect. Moreover, you must be clear that you expect to be treated in a respectful manner by all of the people in your life — spouse, parents, children, friends, people at work, even strangers.

People who are critical of others feel unloved and therefore they see others as unlovable. Their judgments about others constitute personal illusions that cloud their consciousness and degrade the quality of their lives. They think their perceptions have something to say about the people they are judging, but it is not so. Their judgments, criticisms, complaints, and attacks say a great deal about their own consciousness and very little, if anything, about someone else's.

If someone acts in a judgmental, critical or attacking way toward you, please tell that person immediately how you are feeling. Do so without blaming or attacking back, but ask clearly to be treated respectfully. That is your right. And that is the other person's responsibility.

Don't allow someone to treat you in an unkind or an unfair way without standing up for yourself. Mind you, I am not telling you to attack back or retaliate. I am simply telling you to stand up for yourself and insist that you be treated with respect. When you turn the other cheek, you are telling your abuser to think again and make a different choice.

The important thing is to oppose what is disrespectful when it happens. Otherwise you will feel resentful and entitled to make judgments of the person who criticized or attacked you. That, as you know, is passive/aggressive. Retaliating slowly over time is no better than retaliating in the heat of the moment. The key is not to retaliate at all, but to stand up for yourself clearly and forcefully without impugning the dignity of the other person.

Unless you know in the core of your being that you deserve to be treated kindly, you will put up with unnecessary abuse and allow yourself to become a victim. Being a victim who gives power away to others is not spiritual. It is irresponsible to yourself and to the other person.

You do not empower another by giving your power to him. Instead, you give him a false sense of responsibility and control, which prevents him from taking appropriate responsibility for his own life. This arrangement is co-dependent and mutually invalidating. When one person does not carry her own weight, the other person has to carry his weight as well as the weight of the other person. The result is that both people — not just the person who gave her power away — become weak, tired, discouraged and resentful.

For a relationship between two people to work, each person must take responsibility for treating the other with dignity and respect. This creates a foundation of trust and mutual regard, on which genuine equality can be built.

Forgiveness

In any intimate relationship, no matter how good it is, people forget to honor each other. They get stressed out and project their pain onto each other. They attack and defend, give and receive guilt, and generally make a mess of things. I want you to know this not so you can make excuses for yourself, but so you will not give up on your relationship when it is asking you to grow in wisdom and emotional strength.

Your intimate partnership is a microcosm of your entire journey which, as you know, is played out in relationship with others. Since there are no perfect partners out there, your challenge is to accept and honor the imperfect one who stands before you and, yes, to honor yourself, even though your life also is riddled with mistakes.

If you and your partner can forgive each other's transgressions and reestablish your trust in one another, then you can deepen in your love and your capacity for intimacy. This is the challenging part of relationship.

Anyone can enter into relationship. Falling in love

is easy, especially when hormones are at work. And leaving isn't much harder, especially when people are blindly projecting their fears onto each other. But what most people don't seem to be willing to do is to practice forgiveness together. And that is why so many partnerships fail.

Forgiveness is the key to success in every relationship. Indeed, if you and another person are committed to practicing forgiveness you can live together successfully, even if you don't have a lot in common.

On the other hand, if the two of you are not willing to practice forgiveness, then nothing you try will work. No, not religion, or psychotherapy, or relationship workshops. If one of you is willing and the other is not, then the odds are a little better, but still not so good, unless the willing one sets such a strong example that the unwilling one becomes willing. While one person can practice forgiveness, and this is always helpful, it takes two to heal the wounds of mutual trespass.

If you decide to leave one relationship because you are unwilling to forgive, what makes you think that you can succeed in another? It's true, people are different and some people push your buttons more than others, but everyone is imperfect and everyone is going to push your buttons at one time or other. Your ability to create a successful relationship depends not so much on your choice of partner, but on your willingness to forgive yourself and the partner you choose.

By all means, hold out for the partner you want. Insist on common goals, shared interests and mutual attraction. Abandon any relationship that promises to be abusive, even though you might eventually learn something there. Don't play the game of love with half a deck.

But realize, my friends, that no matter how well or how poorly you choose a mate, the practice of forgiveness will be necessary. It is the one constant. It is the key to your ultimate happiness and that of your partner.

Through the practice of forgiveness, imperfect people become whole, and broken relationships are healed and strengthened. Through the practice of forgiveness, you learn what real love and real essence are all about. Through your forgiveness, your mate is transformed into the Beloved, the perfect teacher come to set you free of judgments and illusions.

That synergy of lover and beloved is the great promise of relationship. When two people surrender fully to their union, they become one in heart and mind. Their greatest delight is to serve each other. Entwined in everlasting embrace, they become the nurturing Mother and empowering Father, redeeming all wounded children from the suffering of the past, reaching out to all beings with the message of love and forgiveness, uplifting souls and helping them accept the profound opportunity for intimacy that this journey offers us.

Validation

As soon as you and your partner want something different, correction is needed. You are already off track. It's time to stop, take a deep breath, step back and look at what's happening. Ask yourself "How did we polarize? What fear is coming up for me? What do I want honored that I don't think is being honored here?"

Don't blame yourself or the other person. Don't try to be right or make the other person wrong. Just acknowledge the separation you feel and the belief that you and your partner want different outcomes. Understand and agree together that this separation cannot be bridged while fear is coming up for one or both people.

Take some time alone and get clear about what

you are afraid of, what you feel you need to defend, what your hurt or anger is about. And try to tune into what positive reassurance or affirmation you need from your partner. Then, when you are both feeling peaceful, take turns asking each other directly for the desired validation.

Almost all fear, anger, and hurt stem from your feeling unloved or unappreciated. When someone acts in a way that pushes your buttons, you interpret that behavior as meaning that the person doesn't care. When you respond in a hurt or angry way, the other person feels invalidated by you. The downward spiral of mutual attack and invalidation continues until you are both thoroughly disgusted with each other. Yet this is a game that you both agree to play, although probably not consciously.

When you recognize that you and your partner are moving into the game of "I'll hurt you because you hurt me," you must stop immediately. Tell your partner..."I don't want to do this. Let's take some time to tune into what's going on inside before this situation escalates beyond control and we turn off our love completely."

Just stop and say "I'm going to take a walk. I'll be back when I understand better what's happening inside. I want to talk with you when I'm feeling okay, not when I'm feeling hurt or angry."

When you walk, realize that what you are feeling — unloved and unappreciated — goes very deep. It is not just a response to this particular incident with your partner. It is a response to every experience you've ever had in which you felt attacked, judged, rejected, abandoned, or betrayed. When the emotional body is triggered, even though the trigger seems insignificant, many past memories and levels of experience are contacted. The sadness that comes from feeling the loss of love can be intense.

Obviously, your partner is not responsible for the depth of sadness you feel. S/he was just the trigger. So take him or her off the hook, and see that the job of bringing love to the sad and wounded parts of you belongs primarily to you. Spend some time being gentle and loving with yourself. Understand that all you want from your partner is reassurance that s/he loves you and wants to be with you. When you return to your partner, ask for that reassurance. Ask for specific words that will help you remember that you are loved. Ask for a hug, some cuddling, a backrub, or some eye contact.

Listen to what your partner needs from you. And, remember, the issue is always that s/he needs to feel loved and accepted by you, whatever the specific request for validation is.

When you and your partner have difficulty validating each other, the relationship goes into crisis. When you criticize and invalidate each other, negative patterns are set into motion which destroy the trust and block the love you and your partner have for each other.

Of course, it is not realistic to expect that you can completely validate another human being, especially when that person is insecure and needy. People who have not learned to validate themselves have a very difficult time in relationships. They expect more attention and approval than most people are capable of giving. That means they are rejected a lot, and that only adds to their insecurity.

There are many times in the course of a relationship when you and your partner may appear to want different things. But that is just the symptom of a more radical problem. If you look deeply enough, you will see that neither one of you feels validated by the other.

If you felt validated, you would feel safe in the relationship and empowered to explore your differences without threatening each other. Because you felt loved by the other person and wanted to maintain that love, you would not take a rigid position when disagreements arise. Instead, you would look together for ways in which both of you could meet your needs and receive the validation that is important to you.

When love is present in a relationship, the question is always "What are *we* going to do?" not "What am *I* going to do?" Both people want what is best for the relationship, what keeps them connected to love. Finding that shared reality is both the challenge and the reward of every committed relationship. In the process, both people grow beyond narrow self-interest and learn to serve the higher purpose of their union.

VII
Staying Connected to Love

When love is present, the body and the world
are lifted up. They are infused with light, possibility
and celebration of goodness. The world you see
when Spirit is present in your heart and your life
is not the same world that you see
when you are preoccupied with your ego needs.

Self and Persona

Love is omnipresent in the universe, yet you have a hard time staying connected to it. Why is this?

The reason you don't feel connected to love is that you believe that there is something wrong with you. You are afraid of being judged or rejected by others.

You feel that you are not acceptable as you are because, for most of your life, you have accepted other people's ideas and opinions as the truth about you. Yet what mother, dad, teacher, minister said about you is just their opinion. Some of it might have been accurate at one time in your life, but even that part might not be accurate now.

Unfortunately, you internalize the feedback you get from others. And you develop your self image based on it. In other words, your opinion of yourself is not based on what you know and find out about you, but on what other people tell you.

The *you* you know is a creation of other people's beliefs and judgments which you accept as true about yourself. Even your so-called "personality" is a set of behavior patterns you adopted to accommodate the behavior of significant others in your life.

Where then is the "real you" in the equation of

self and other? The real you is the unknown factor, the essence that has been heavily clothed in the judgments and interpretations which you have accepted about yourself and your experience.

This is true for everyone, not just for you. People relate to one another not as authentic, self-realized beings, but as personae, masks, roles, identities. Often, people have more than one mask that they wear, depending on whom they are with and what is expected of them.

The true Self gets lost and forgotten among all these disguises. And its great gift of authenticity is not consciously acknowledged.

The true Self knows that you are inherently good, acceptable, capable of giving and receiving love. It knows that anything is possible if you believe deeply enough in yourself.

The true Self is not bound by the limitations, judgments and interpretations that the persona lives with. Indeed, it can be said that Self and persona live in different worlds. The world of Self is bright and self-fulfilling. The world of persona is dark and light is sought from others.

Self says "I am." Persona says "I am this" or "I am that." Self lives and expresses unconditionally. Persona lives and expresses conditionally. Self is motivated by love and says "I can." Persona lives in fear and says "I can't." Persona complains, apologizes and makes excuses. Self accepts, integrates and gives its gift.

You are Self, but believe yourself to be your persona. As long as you operate as persona, you will have experiences that confirm your beliefs about yourself and others. When you realize that all personae are just masks you and others have agreed to wear, you will learn to see behind the masks.

When that happens, you will glimpse the radiance of the Self within and without. You will see a bright being, eminently worthy and capable of love, dynamically creative, generous and self-fulfilling. That is your inmost nature. And that is the nature of all beings in your experience.

When you accept who you really are, your arguments with others cease. For you no longer do battle with their personae. You see the light behind the mask. Your light and their light are all that matter.

When you contact the truth about you, you recognize that a great deal that you have come to accept about you is false. You are not better or worse than others. You are not stupid, or brilliant, or handsome, or ugly. Those are just judgments someone made that you accepted. None of them is true.

When you know the truth about you, you know that you are not your body, although you need to accept it and take care of it. You are not your thoughts and feelings, although you need to be aware of them and see how they are creating the drama of your life. You are not the roles that you are playing — husband or wife, mother or father, son or daughter, employee or boss, secretary or plumber — although you need to make peace with whatever role you choose to play. You are not anything external. You are not anything that can be defined by something or someone else.

The purpose of your journey here is to discover the Self and leave the persona behind. You are here to find out that the Source of love lies within your own consciousness. You do not have to seek love outside of yourself. Indeed, the very act of seeking it in the world will prevent you from recognizing it within yourself. And if you can't find love within, you will never be able to find it in others.

You can't see the light in others until you see it in yourself. Once you see it in yourself, there is no one in whom you do not see the light. It does not matter if they see it or not. You know it's there. And it is the light you address when you speak to them.

The world of personae is a chaotic and reactive

world. It is fueled by fear and judgment. It is real only because you and others believe in it and define yourselves by the conditions you find there. But those conditions are not ultimate reality. They are simply a collective drama of your making. Yes, the drama has its own rules, its costumes, its inter-relationships and its plan of action. But none of this matters when you take your costume off and step off the stage.

Mind you, the play will go on. It does not depend on you alone. But when you know it's just a play, you can choose to participate in it or not. If you participate, you will do so remembering who you are, understanding the part that you play without being attached to it.

Suffering ends when your attachment to all conditions dissolves. Then, you rest in the Self, the embodiment of love, the Source of creation itself.

Who Is the Christ?

The Self is all-powerful. The persona is not. The only reason persona seems to be powerful is because Self is invested in it. In the same way, the breath is all powerful. The body is not. The only reason the body is powerful is because the breath is invested in it.

The body is a temporary container for breath. The persona is a temporary container for Self. Breath and Self are deeper than any experience or set of conditions. They arise inwardly and thus cannot be defined externally.

When you breathe deeply, you let go of the tension that creates dis-ease in the body. Rhythmic breathing takes you into a state of physical ecstasy. When you remember Self, you go beyond your attachment to the idiosyncrasies of your persona. You experience a peace and a freedom that lies beyond the conditions that appear to bind you.

As Self, you are never a prisoner of conditions. How could you be? If you see yourself as a prisoner or a hapless victim, you are in your persona. When you dwell in your Self, you know yourself to be totally innocent and free, regardless of what others may believe about you.

Christ can be crucified, but he cannot be forced to hate those who attack him. He stands committed in his love, regardless of the hatred that dwells in other people's hearts. Christ is gentle with himself and all others, yet he will defend the truth fearlessly. No one can intimidate him, nor would he intimidate any brother or sister. His only call to his siblings is a call to awaken and accept the mantle of love.

Do not think that I alone am Christ or you will miss the entire point of my teaching. Every one of you is the anointed one. Every one of you is chosen.

But to be chosen is not enough. My Jewish brothers and sisters were chosen, yet they chose to worship idols nonetheless. My Christian brothers and sisters were chosen, yet they chose to make a mockery of my teachings. You see, it is not enough to be chosen. You too must choose. Will you walk the path that opens before you or be drawn astray?

Other paths will always promise more but deliver less. And you may be tempted to try those paths. That is okay. I do not condemn you for seeking a short cut. Only realize when you come to a dead end, and turn around. You can retrace your steps and pick up where you left off if you are determined enough.

I never demanded that you be perfect. I too was not perfect, although you believe me to be. That, of course, is the problem. If I am perfect, then you must be. And if you are not perfect, then you believe that you have failed me and yourself. That is pure foolishness. Please discard these erroneous ideas. Accept yourself as you are, with all your mistakes and apparent weaknesses. Then you will be ready to walk the path with me.

Confession and Atonement

Why do you suppose I asked you to confess your sins? Do you honestly think it is because I wanted to give some priest artificial power over you so that you would have to beg forgiveness from him and from the authority of the Church? What nonsense! Never would I ask you to seek forgiveness from anyone other than the God who dwells within your heart.

Please understand. I asked you to confess your sins so that you might lighten your load, so that you might release the judgments you make about self and others. You cannot walk next to me so long as you carry those judgments with you. They are too heavy a load. You cannot take them where you and I must go together.

So confess your sins and your pain in a private place where no other man or woman enters. Forgive your mistakes. Vow to learn and to do better by yourself and others. Connect to love in the private place where you pray and confess, and take that love with you when you leave. Find this inner temple when you become burdened by the affairs of the world and your attachment to them.

Come and take sanctuary here. Come and release your worries, your fears, your guilt about what you have said and done. Come and let your heart be mended so that you can go forth and make amends with anyone you have slighted and treated unkindly. Come and find peace, so that you can go forth and make peace with your brothers and sisters.

I asked you to confess your sins, not to hold onto them. I asked you to forgive yourself, not to let some priestly hierarchy hold you in perpetual bondage.

If you have been holding yourself prisoner, know now my brother or sister, it is time to set yourself free. No matter what you have said or done, you do not deserve to suffer. Your suffering will not feed the hungry or heal the sick.

No, my dear friend, come and take the forgiveness I offer you so that you can come back into your life with a clear vision and a strong heart. I offer you freedom, not for yourself alone, but for the sake of all those who need your love and your service.

Come and rededicate yourself to the purpose for which you came. If you have acted in an unloving way, then it is imperative that you release yourself from guilt, from excuses and victimhood. Come and take the branch of peace and carry it forth into the neighborhoods you know, where people need empowerment and hope. Your love can heal all the wounds of the past, if you will only believe in yourself and believe in others.

Holding yourself in chains will do no good for you or anyone else. Come and accept my forgiveness that you may offer it to others and be a force for healing and reconciliation. Nothing else can bring you joy or redemption.

Do not let the world tell you who you are. For you are not what others tell you, even if you appear to be fulfilling their expectations. Consider it well, my friend, do you want to continue to live in fear and sorrow, just because others expect you to be hard and tough? Will you squander your life just to protect an image that someone else gave you long ago?

I say no, brother; no, sister. It is time to cast that image away. It is not who you are. It will not bring you peace or happiness. Let it go. And let me help you learn of yourself anew.

When I went forth to serve my brothers and sisters, I took the name Emmanuel so that I would always remember that God was with me. By constantly remembering God, I was able to see my innocence, as well as the innocence and purity of all of the beings I beheld on my journey.

You must do the same. You must carry God with you in your heart and remember that your only purpose here on earth is to accept your innocence and to help others accept theirs. That is why you have come to me. And I will use everything that you bring to me. If you have been a criminal, a drug dealer, an alcoholic, a prostitute, a corrupt preacher or politician, I will use all of that. I will send you back amongst the people whose fears and habits you know and together we will bring them home. No, not by condemning their actions or trying to fix them, but by loving them, seeing them whole, and reminding them of the truth about themselves, which they have forgotten.

Conversion

When you are secure in your own experience of the divine, you do not need to convince anyone else to believe as you do. Yet, because your experience is significant for you, you are happy to share it with others.

Nevertheless, you must understand that you are helpful to others only to the extent that you encourage them to use whatever portions of your testimony are uplifting and empowering to them. They must decide what is helpful and what is not, not you.

When you seek to impose your beliefs and opinions onto others, you are not respecting their right to decide what works for them. This is manipulation, not ministry.

So much value is placed on words and concepts, yet I tell you this is not where the experience of conversion happens. Conversion happens primarily in the heart, and not so much in the mind.

People are not converted to some concept of God, but to an experience of love. One who does not believe in something beyond his small ego suddenly opens to a loving presence that exists both in him and in others. That is the experience that changes lives, that helps people accept and honor themselves at the deepest level.

People are not converted to the power of love by adopting a set of beliefs and parroting them to others. It does not happen through proselytizing. It does not happen when you make others wrong and try to get them to adopt "the right teaching."

People are converted to the power of love when you love and accept them unconditionally. That means that it doesn't matter to you what they believe. It doesn't matter how they dress, what songs they sing, or how they bury their dead. All that is immaterial.

When you can love and accept people exactly as they are, then you become a true minister of God, a genuine brother or sister. You don't need to change their beliefs or customs, or fix their lives. You just need to demonstrate the power of love in the way that you speak and act toward them. That is what gets their attention.

No one can resist a person who radiates love. Everyone comes to sit at his or her feet.

Can you imagine that? These people are not even invited, never mind proselytized, yet they come anyway. They come because love calls to them and they respond.

You do not have to go out aggressively to spread my message. You do not have to hit people over the head with it and drag them back to your churches or synagogues. Just love each other, and people will come. Keep the love going, and the people will keep coming.

They will come and fill themselves to the brim, and they will return to wherever they have come from with their cup running over. That is the way my teaching spreads. Being a minister of love is effortless. You just keep loving, and people keep coming. You keep admitting your mistakes and confessing your worries and fears, and people hold you ever more deeply in their hearts.

You do not have to be perfect to be a mouthpiece for my teaching, but you do need to be humble. You have to meet people where they are. And you need to be honest about where you are. Pretense will not work. If you lie to yourself, you will lie to others, and if you lie to others, you will eventually be found out. So save yourself some valuable time and tell the truth from the beginning.

No one is perfect. I am no more perfect than you, and you are no more perfect than the least of your brothers or sisters. Every one of you makes mistakes. Every one of you has much to learn about giving and receiving love.

We don't get to heaven by pretending to be there when we aren't, nor do we get there by pretending that we have some impossible handicap. Heaven is available to all who are willing to learn about love.

Are you willing to keep learning? If so, the doors of heaven will keep opening to you. Every time you walk through one door, another one will open. For there are many rooms in the house of love. And each room must be explored fully.

When you begin to let love into your heart, the process of exploration ceases to be work and drudgery. On the contrary, it becomes energetic and fun. You discover that you have many gifts that you can share with others along the way. And you learn to receive the gifts that others need to share with you.

Do not look down on or despise another's gift. Even if it doesn't seem to measure up, please accept it anyway. Look into your brother's eyes and see how much he wishes to give the gift, and you cannot refuse to accept it.

After all, what do you know about the gift? If God hands you a frog, are you going to toss it back in the pond when you know that frogs can turn into princes? That, my friends would not be wise.

Please allow for surprises. The greatest gifts often come when you least expect them.

Living the Miracle

I hate to contradict one of your favorite slogans, but "expecting a miracle" is not always helpful. Sometimes you think you need a miracle, but all you need is a little common sense. Sometimes, you are certain you need a miracle, but all you need to do is walk through your fear.

I'm not trying to suggest that there is a shortage of miracles out there and that you must save them up for special occasions. On the contrary, there are miracles happening everywhere, but you often don't see them because you are expecting fireworks.

When you are doing the best that you can in your life, you are making miracles constantly. When you are moving through your fear, seeing your projections, and reaching out lovingly to people who are dispirited or afraid, you are a miracle worker.

But, if you are smart, you don't call yourself a miracle worker. You don't call attention to yourself. You let others whom you empower and uplift take the credit: "You see what you did with God's help...isn't that fantastic!" You help people build up their confidence so that they can learn to make their own miracles.

Some of you think that God does all the work. But I hate to disappoint you. You do 90% of the work in every miracle that transpires. God does just 10%. God inspires you and guides you, but you do the work. Yet you cannot take credit for the work you do in God's name. You need to give God the credit, even though you did 90% of the work.

Why is that? Because you do not want people to become attached to you. You want them to understand that the God that lies within their own hearts is the one who makes everything happen. Then they will begin to listen. And when they feel divine inspiration within, they will act on it. They will put all of their energies behind it, and so they will make their own miracles and pass them along to others.

I could have taken credit for the healings that happened in my presence, but I did not. For I was just the force that catalyzed these movements of healing and forgiveness. The faith that people had in me they learned to find in themselves. I gave people back to God. I did not ask for a following.

Nor do I want one now. Please don't go around saying "Jesus says this and Jesus says that." Forget Jesus. Just be a loving, accepting presence, and others will come home to the true Self through you.

You see, it does not matter who the door is. It could be me. It could be you. It could be another brother or sister. The door does not need to be celebrated.

When the door needs to be celebrated, it ceases to be a door. When people grasp the finger pointing to the moon, they can no longer tell where it is pointing.

Don't make yourself important. Let the glory go to others and you will be glorified truly. You will experience the ecstasy of being the door that opens when people knock. And I assure you there is no greater ecstasy than that.

When you do not call attention to yourself, you become capable of working deeply in every moment. No one interferes with your work. Indeed, only the most discerning notice what you do.

It is a rare person who can go about her work

without calling attention to herself, without seeking publicity, without building an organization around her. It is a rare person who inspires without taking credit, who heals without charging a fee and gives without asking anything in return. You may seek her, but you will find her only if you are prepared to walk in her footsteps.

The greatest teachers are the most humble, the most loving, the most empowering to others. If you wish to find such a teacher, you must look beyond appearances. Find the man or woman who promises you nothing, but loves you without hesitation. Find the teacher who makes no pretension to fix or to teach, yet who opens your heart when s/he looks into your eyes.

When you think of great teachers, you think of glitter, flowing robes and great crowds of people gathered together. But none of these trappings are required. Indeed, they often get in the way. The focus goes onto the Guru, instead of onto the aspirant. But it is the aspirant who must wake up, not the Guru.

One day, I am going to create a rest home for Gurus. I'm going to call them to a beautiful spot in the Andes, or the Himalayas, where they can keep busy playing bocci or shuffleboard and stop causing so much trouble.

Without authority figures out there to inspire or validate you, you will have to pay more attention to your own experience and guidance. You will have to stop looking for fireworks and work with the warp and woof of your life. You will learn to accept the unfolding tapestry, mistakes and all.

No matter how tuned in, accomplished, or holy you are, life is not going to unfold the way you expect it to. Sometimes a hidden challenge will surface and require all your love, patience or attention. At other times, an unexpected gift may arrive like a hummingbird appearing magically at the feeder outside your window.

There are ups and downs on the journey. But the ups are not always up, and the downs are not always down. Buddha knew this. And you will learn it too. Just stay steady in your life.

Don't expect a miracle. No, no, no. Don't expect anything. Just be with what happens as best you can.

VIII
The Ties that Bind

You will experience many small deaths in the course of your life, many times when you must let go of the arms that once comforted you and walk alone into the uncertain future. Every time you do so your fears will rise up and you will have to walk through them. Learning to let go is one of the great lessons of this embodiment. With letting go comes a new freedom for you. That is what it means to be born again.

The Language of Fear

When you see another as less than yourself, you are seeing through your fear. And fear, as you know, is blind.

No one is less worthy than you, even if that person's behavior toward you is unwarranted and objectionable. His fear makes him act toward you in a belligerent way. Your fear makes you think of him and act toward him in an equally belligerent way. Fear in one person tends to invoke fear in another. That is the equation of mutual trespass.

The only way out of the cycle of mutual attack and defense is to see your attacker as he really is. When you see him as a decent human being who is responding to you out of fear, you can speak and act in a way that will lessen his fear. That means you don't attack back. It does not mean that you allow the other person to intimidate you.

Each of you must find a way to stand up lovingly for yourself without putting other people down. Your regard for yourself is essential. It is precisely that self-regard that must extend to include the other person.

Extending your love in the face of someone else's

fear is the most difficult thing you will ever have to do. Yet it is essential that you learn this.

There are so many people who are afraid and are acting out in angry ways, you are bound to run across someone like this. I'm not just talking about murderers, thieves, and rapists. I'm talking about people who cut you off in traffic, call you names, push you on the sidewalk, threaten to take you to court, or spread untrue rumors about you.

Many people are time bombs of anger waiting to explode. If you engage with them in an uncentered way, you can trigger their rage.

To handle these situations skillfully, do your best to refrain from making judgments about others and try to keep your heart open to them, even when they treat you unfairly. By all means let them know that you want to be treated with respect, but offer them the same respect when you confront them.

Don't confront people out of anger. When you react in an angry or defensive way to someone's attack, you will only make the situation worse.

Before you respond, call time out and give yourself a chance to look at your options. Which response is empowering to you without threatening the other person? Which response honors both of you?

You do not have to respond to the fearful words

and actions of other people. You can respond to what lies behind their words and actions. You can give them the love and respect they are seeking from you. When they feel that from you, their hostility toward you will cease.

I never said that this path would be easy. There are real challenges here which you must learn to meet. You too become fearful and act in hostile ways toward others who don't deserve your anger or your blame. You must learn to apologize to others for these attacking behaviors. You must see the times when you are callous and unloving and take responsibility for treating people with greater gentleness and respect.

This is a two-way street. Everyone who has been mistreated by another has mistreated others at one time or another. All of you have the same lessons to learn in this regard.

Leaving Home/Coming Home

If you think that I or anyone else has something you don't have, you are already giving your power away. In the words of the Negro spiritual, "You have the whole world in your hands." Nothing is missing in you whatsoever. Whatever you need you will find if you believe in yourself.

But first, learn to trust yourself and the infinite resources that are available to you as a spiritual being. Do not limit the possibilities that lie before you. Do not shut the doors of opportunity with negative thinking. Be open. Be willing.

Let go of your specific expectations, but hold onto the general expectation and belief that your needs will be met in ways that you cannot even begin to understand. Be surrendered. Rest in your faith that God has only good things for you. Know that even the tests and the lessons are there to make you stronger and more flexible in your ability to love.

Let God be your teacher. Let the Tao flower in you. You don't need to control things anymore. When you are willing to be helpful, life flows through you. You become the channel, the means by which love without conditions can reach into the world.

Do not give your power away to others. Nobody else knows what is good for you. Nobody else knows what your mission here is all about. Stay away from psychics, teachers, therapists and gurus who would direct your life through their own limited beliefs about themselves and you.

You have everything you need to be guided

wisely in your life. Trust in this. Trust in your connection to the Source of all things. You are no further away from God than I am. You don't need me to bring you to the feet of the Divine. You don't need your partner or your teacher to bring you there. You are already there.

God is incapable of moving away from you. God is ever-present in your life. When you do not feel the presence, it is because you have moved away. You have given your power to some earthly authority. You have left the place of the indwelling God in search of something special in the world. That search always comes up empty, but that doesn't mean that you won't keep trying to find the answer somewhere outside of yourself.

Many of you think that I want your exclusive allegiance. Nothing could be further from the truth. When I ask you to believe in me, it is to empower yourself, to know that you can do as I have done, to see your greatness. But you can do this directly and dispense with me. I am not necessary to your resurrection. You are the lamb of God. You are the one who has come to forgive yourself and release the world from her chains of envy and regret.

If you have a teacher who empowers you, I am happy. It does not matter to me if that teacher is a

Buddhist or a Jew, a Christian or a Moslem, a shaman or a businessman. If you are learning to trust yourself, if you are becoming more open in your mind and your heart, then I am happy for you. It does not matter what specific path you are on, what symbols you believe in, or what scrolls you consider sacred. I look to the fruit of all those beliefs and endeavors to see if you are stepping into your divinity or giving that power away to someone or something outside yourself.

No, I do not want your exclusive allegiance. I simply ask you to choose a teacher and a teaching which empowers you to discover truth within your own heart, for there alone will you find it. When you give your power away, to me or to anyone else, I know that you have not heard me.

How many times have I told you I am not the only son or daughter of God? All of you share that lineage with me. We are God's children. We carry divine love and wisdom within us. All the answers to our problems lie within us.

I stand before you as a model of one who realized his divinity while living in a body in this world. I demonstrate to you the power that manifests when one listens to one's inner voice and follows it, even when other people judge or object. I stand for the inner authority of the universal heart-mind which holds everyone in equal reverence. I know that when you trust the divine within, you cannot help but become authentic.

I have tried to show you a way of cutting yourself loose from parental authority, cultural authority, religious authority. I have tried to tell you that who you are is far greater than all that. I have told you that the laws and customs of men and women are limited by the conditions of their experience. They cannot see beyond them.

But there is a Reality that is beyond that narrow subjective reality. And you can find it, from the inside out, for it is the very ground of your being. It is who you are when you strip away all the false beliefs you have accepted from parents, family, culture and church or synagogue.

I have asked you to have the courage to stand alone so you could step into your life and shed the narrow identifications which prevent you from knowing who you are. I have asked you to leave your homes and your work, so that you could stand back and look at your life from a distance, seeing the self-limiting, the fear-based patterns of relating. I have asked you to stand back so that you would realize that you do not have to sell yourself short.

You do not have to give your power away to customs and traditions that don't honor your spiritual roots and branches.

A man and a woman must leave the home of their parents and open to new experiences if they are to create a home of their own that will not repeat the negative family patterns. For the same reason, you must leave your school, your career, your religion, and your relationship so that you can discover who you are apart from the conditions which the structures of life place on you.

You are not just a son or a daughter, a husband or a wife, a carpenter or a plumber, a black person or a white person, a Christian or a Jew. You are much more than any of that. Yet if you identify with these roles, you will not discover the essence within you that goes beyond them. Nor will you find a way to transcend the inevitable division these external definitions will create in your life.

I have asked you to leave home so that you could one day return knowing what "home" really is. I have asked you to go on a pilgrimage in which you shed your external identity so that you can discover what your true identity is. I have asked you to listen to others with respect, but never to accept their ideas and opinions as an authority in your life. I have asked you to find that authority within, even though no one else in your life agrees with it, and I have asked you to follow that inner authority even in the face of outright criticism from your friends, your family, your church, your race, your political party, and your country.

I have asked you to stand alone, not because I wish to isolate you, but so you can know the truth and anchor in it. For there will be times when you will have to stand in that truth in the midst of a crowd of people who would ignore it, scapegoating and condemning their brothers and sisters, as they once condemned me. There will be times, my friend, when you will be the voice in the wilderness that helps people find their way back home. And you could not become that voice if you did not leave home, if you did not learn to stand alone with the truth.

When you know how to stand alone, it is easy to stand with others who uphold their own truth. You aren't threatened by what they believe or what their experience is. You honor all that. You honor every authentic path to divine wisdom and love. And you take great delight in being with people who are comfortable being themselves.

Letting Go

Most external changes follow on internal shifts of allegiance and attention. When one ceases to be committed to a relationship or a course of action, a shift takes place. Energy is withdrawn from one direction and placed in a new direction.

You can argue until you are blue in the face about whether it is right or wrong that someone's commitment changes, but it won't do you any good. You cannot prevent other people from going forward in their growth, even if you don't agree with their decisions.

Don't play the role of martyr. If you look deeply enough, you will see that every apparent "loss" you experience brings an unexpected gain. When one person leaves a relationship that is not growing into deeper intimacy, the other person is set free too. But s/he must be willing to let go to appreciate the gift of freedom which has been offered.

Wanting someone who doesn't want you is a way of punishing yourself. After a while, you will get tired of your masochism and realize that you have other choices about where to put your energy.

When you cease to be committed to your career, it falls apart. When you stop being committed to your relationship, it begins to crumble. It is no longer as nurturing, as supportive, as fun as it used to be. You can blame this change on your partner or your boss, but you will be missing the whole point. The relationship or the career no longer works because you are no longer giving it your love, your support, your commitment.

Neither holding onto the other person nor blaming him or her will help you get on with your life. If you don't want to live your life in the shadow of a ruptured union, where negative emotions are constantly recycled, you must learn to let go.

Perhaps the greatest gift that you can ever give to yourself is to set someone or something you love free. Staying in a relationship which does not have the full commitment of both people is not constructive for either person. Either mutual commitment must be re-established or the process of letting go must begin in earnest.

When something in your life is not working, you often try first to fix it. Then, if that doesn't work, you may pretend for a while that it's fixed even though you know it isn't. Finally, you realize that your play-acting isn't fooling anyone and that your heart just isn't in it. That's when you are ready to learn to let go.

As long as you hold onto a role or relationship that

has served its purpose in your life, you will be holding yourself hostage to the past. Letting go is an act of substantial courage. There is always some degree of pain in the release of someone or something that once brought you joy and happiness. You will have to be patient and mourn the loss. But when your mourning is over, you will arise as a new person. You will open to opportunities you never could have dreamed of. As you explore these new opportunities, you will step back into your life with confidence and faith. Your life will be renewed and you will be reborn as the phoenix is from the ashes of the past.

The fire of change is never easy to weather. But if you surrender, the conflagration is quickly over. In the enriched soil, the seeds of tomorrow can be sown.

I have told you that unless you die and be reborn you cannot enter the kingdom of heaven. No one comes here to earth without suffering the pain of loss. Every identity you assume will be taken from you when it is time. Every person you love will die. It is just a matter of time. And it is just a matter of time before you too leave your body and the world behind.

All sacred teachings exhort you not to be attached to the things of this world, because they are not permanent. Yet you get attached nonetheless. That is part of the process of your awakening.

Getting attached and letting go. Embracing and releasing. Personally, I don't think it is necessary to avoid attachments. But it is essential to realize when they become dysfunctional. When certain ties bind, you have no choice but to give them up. Learning to let go is one of the great lessons of this embodiment.

With letting go comes a new freedom for you. That is what it means to be born again.

You will experience many small deaths in the course of your life, many times when you must let go of the arms that once comforted you and walk alone into the uncertain future. Every time you do so your fears will rise up and you will have to walk through them. Often, you will believe that if you let go you will die, but you will find out otherwise. When you let go of what no longer works, you are guided to what does.

Don't be impatient. No one is reborn instantaneously. It takes time. It is a process. Just know that the more that you surrender, the easier it will be for you.

The tide goes out and comes back in. People let go of one attachment only to form another one which challenges them more. Life is rhythmic, but progressive. As earth and water breathe together, the shape of the beach changes. Storms come and go.

In the end, a profound peace comes and pervades the heart and mind. Finally, the ground of being has been reached. Here the changing waters come and go, and the earth delights in them as a lover delights in the playful touch of his beloved.

A deep acceptance is felt and, with it, a quiet recognition that all things are perfect as they are. This is grace, the presence of God come to dwell in your heart and in your life.

Change and the Changeless

Although some things change, other things never do. Thoughts change, emotions change, houses and jobs change, bodies change, the world changes. But the core of you does not change.

On the surface, each one of you looks different. Differences in physical appearance, personality, temperament, culture, religion, national heritage, all contribute to your uniqueness. As long as individuals respect one another, the diversity created by individual uniqueness is a positive phenomenon.

Growth too is a unique proposition. People grow in different ways. Experience teaches some people to be more assertive and others to be less. Some people grow to become more gregarious; others learn how to be happy alone.

But everyone who is here needs to breathe air, to eat, to drink water. Every person needs acceptance and love to flower. When people are nurtured physically, emotionally, intellectually and spiritually, they are happy and joyful. For this is their natural condition.

When you learn to accept yourself and others just as you are in the present moment, you live in your natural state. You move with life as it unfolds, accepting and working with what is.

Tao flowers in you. You dwell in the universal heart-mind. When you look at two people who live in this place, you know them to be the same, even though they look different. The same light shines in their eyes, even though one has brown eyes and the other green. Both have an easy and relaxed smile, and you feel equally safe being in their presence.

Human nature may be different, but divine nature is the same. When divine nature and human nature blend together in a person's heart/mind, you have all of the strengths of the individual's authentic gifts and temperament without the insecurity, anxiety, and divisiveness of ego consciousness. Each person can be unique without threatening or undermining the uniqueness of anyone else. People can be themselves without trespassing on others.

This blending of the personal and universal is

called by many names: enlightenment, awakening, satori, samadhi, ascension, in-dwelling spirit, etc. It is a state of consciousness that reflects psychological integration and interpersonal harmony. It demonstrates congruence within and without.

All human beings have the potential to dwell in this state of peace and happiness. To do so they simply have to shed the ego-identifications which reinforce their judgments and create struggles with other people.

In this state of consciousness, that which changes and that which does not change come together. This is why it has been called the eternal or deathless state. In this state, individual differences survive without being divisive. One is not attached to what makes one different from others.

And so when the moment of death comes and one is asked to surrender the personal, it is not difficult. One prefers the stillness of the absolute to the chatter of the conditional. One would gladly trade this breath for the breath that does not come and go.

That which changes arises out of the changeless and returns to it. You cannot imagine the point of origin or the point of return, but you have known moments in your life free of self-consciousness or fear, moments when you felt connected to everyone and everything without trying. And those moments give you a clue of what the deathless state is like.

The closer you get to this state when you are in the body, the less you will fear the moment of death. For you have brought the universal into the personal, the divine into the human, the unconditional into the conditional. When the body/mind container is filled by spirit, it expands and breaks apart so that the energy can go where it is most needed.

When your personal journey comes to fruition, your impersonal journey begins. The Divine Presence in which you have your being decides what you will do and where you will go. You are here to love and to serve. You do not need to ask who, where, why or how. Those questions cease to be relevant when you no longer live for yourself alone.

IX
Re-Union

Do not think that I alone am Christ or you will miss the entire point of my teaching. Every one of you is the anointed one. Every one of you is chosen. It does not matter who the door is. It could be me. It could be you. It could be another. The door does not need to be celebrated. When the door needs to be celebrated, it ceases to be a door.

The Divine Partnership

Imagine living with another person without trying to change him or her in any way. Imagine that your only calling is to accept where that person is, at any time, and to accept where you are in that same moment. Imagine not having to put pressure on others to meet your needs or expectations and knowing that others will not put pressure on you.

Imagine that every moment you share with another person is a moment in which you are fully present and attentive to each other. Imagine feeling connected in your heart to your partner in the same way that you feel connected to your own breathing. When your breath becomes shallow, you automatically become aware of it and take a deep breath. When your attention to your partner becomes attenuated, you make eye contact and allow the mutual consciousness of your love to flow back and forth between your minds and hearts.

Imagine that your relationship is a continual dance in which moving in a complementary way is the only goal. Each one of you is constantly making little adjustments so that you can stay together in a comfortable way. None of these adjustments takes much thought. It is just what you do when you are dancing.

Imagine a dance in which each person takes turns leading. Sometimes one person feels the music more deeply than the other and takes the lead. Another time the other person is more tuned in and leads the way. This happens by itself, out of the mutual regard and attunement of the partners, not because of some prearranged agreement about "equal time."

Imagine feeling that your most profound gift as a human being is to honor your partner with every breath and every step. Imagine considering your partner's thoughts and feelings every time you consider your own.

Imagine not thinking of yourself as a separate being any more. Imagine knowing that you are capable of being alone, but that you can never be alone now that you and your partner have joined as one greater consciousness.

Imagine having a "we" awareness, where you once had an "I" awareness. Imagine being as devoted to your partner's comfort, pleasure, and well-being as you are to your own.

Imagine not considering the possibility of disconnecting from your partner as a way of coming into contact with yourself. Imagine understanding that any disconnection with your partner is a disconnection with yourself.

Your unconditional love and acceptance of your partner is your best and easiest pathway to God-communion. With your partner, you learn to be both lover and beloved. You learn to give and receive unconditional love and acceptance.

When you have learned to do this with one person, you become capable of doing it with all people. That is when Christ is born in you, when the one becomes the many and the many become the one. When you become the Christ presence as I did, no one will be excluded from your love. What you give to one, you give to all. What you receive from one, you receive from all.

The Christ Mind is the end of separate thoughts, separate agendas, separate wills. The Christ Heart is the end of disparate feelings and special love. The Christ Consciousness has one thought, one agenda, one will, one love for all beings.

But none of this will mean anything to you until you learn to love one person as you love yourself. For most of you, this is the doorway you will open to divine bliss.

So choose your partner well. If you choose one who dances too slowly, you may be held back. If you choose one who dances too fast, you may break your ankle trying to keep up with her/him. Find a partner who dances at the same speed that you do, one who will complement you and help you realize your potential. Find a partner you can empower and assist. On the wings of your mutual love and acceptance of each other, you and your partner may come as close to the divine as you can come in this lifetime.

Letting Your Partner Be

By now it should be clear to you that it is in your relationships with your brothers and sisters that you will learn and grow the most. Yet relationships are a two-edged sword. They promise bliss, yet bring up the most primitive, unintegrated emotions. They promise companionship, yet challenge you to deal with seemingly irreconcilable differences. They promise an end to loneliness, yet open the door to a deeper aloneness.

You may think of a relationship as a pill you take to bring you relief from boredom or loneliness. But all pills have side effects. For every high you experience, there is a corresponding low.

If you want to avoid the low moments, you should avoid having intimate relationships. Unfortunately, if you do this, you will be avoiding your own psychological and spiritual growth. That growth comes from experiencing the highs and the lows of relationship and everything in between. It comes from experiencing all phases of the other person, just as you must experience all phases of yourself.

For a while, it may seem that you lose yourself in the other person. But this happens only in the early phases of a relationship when you are both idolizing each other. When you live with a person, it doesn't take long for everything that is there to come out on the table.

When that happens, you need every skill you have to prevent the relationship from self-destructing. When your partner's fears and insecurities come to the surface in the relationship, you can either react with your own fears and insecurities, or you can compassionately allow your partner to be with his or her experience.

That sounds easy enough, but it is very difficult to do. To let your partner be when s/he is experiencing fear, doubt, ambivalence, victimhood, or ungrounded fantasies about the future is a tremendous challenge. You must detach from what is being said so that you don't react to it or take it personally. Yet, at the same time, you must keep your heart open, be present, and find a graceful way to shift into something practical and upbeat.

There will be times when each one of you goes unexpectedly adrift and the other one must sail alongside and gently bring him/her back. There will also be times when one of you has been in the harbor far too long and can use the other's help lifting your anchor. As long as you stay out of each other's neurotic patterns, you and your partner can do a great deal to help each other grow as life requires.

Engaging with your partner when s/he is expressing negativity of any kind is deadly to the relationship. Instead, you must look beyond the specific words that are being said and realize that your partner is just asking for your love and reassurance. If you give that, and ignore the rest, you can help bring him/her back on track.

Knowing when to engage and when not to engage your partner is the art of loving. It does not happen over night. These are skills that you learn by making mistakes and being clear that you don't want to repeat them.

Giving your partner space when s/he is determined to stay in a space of victimhood, blame and self-pity is as important as giving praise, encouragement and affection when s/he can receive it. What you don't say or do is as important to the health of your relationship as what you do say or do.

The two most important rules of thumb are: 1) Don't try to fix your partner, even if you think s/he wants you to. 2) Don't feel responsible for your partner's sadness, fear, or anger. When your partner is unhappy, lovingly detach and let your partner be. Don't engage. Don't try to fix. Don't feel responsible. Just let your partner be and have faith that s/he will find a way to reconnect with self and ultimately with you. Until that connection with self is made, your partner will be unable to respond to you in any way that will feel satisfying or nurturing to you.

It is ironic perhaps that one of the greatest skills you learn in relationship is how to let your partner be. And one of your greatest awarenesses is that you are not responsible for your partner's changing moods. You do, however, need to learn to dance with them. Part of that dance is backing away, so that you can come together again when you are both able to be present.

Mirror of Innocence

When the snow falls, it covers ground, plants, trees, houses and roads with a white mantle. Everything looks fresh, new, innocent. Forgiveness comes in the same way, undoing the grievances of the past, replacing judgments with acceptance. In the light of forgiveness, you see your problems and challenges differently. You feel capable of meeting your life just the way it is.

Walking out into the new snow, you leave fresh footprints behind you. No more hiding or pretending to hold back. You have ventured forth boldly and anyone can follow you.

Forgiveness is as far-reaching as a snow. It reaches out and touches everything in your life, everything in your heart or your mind.

For forgiveness to bless you, you must be willing to receive it, as the ground receives the snowfall. You must be willing to be occupied and cleansed by something greater than yourself.

In every successful relationship, forgiveness is an ongoing practice. It is a daily, weekly, monthly cleansing. Without forgiveness, there can be no communion between you and your partner. Instead, old wounds will be aggravated by hidden resentments.

This will not do. Negative thoughts and feeling states must be cleared on no less than a daily basis. Do not go to sleep angry at each other. Do not let the sun rise or set without making peace with each other and embracing deeply. The sacredness of your union must be nurtured and celebrated. Give it the time it deserves. Be ready to let go of thoughts and feelings that can only injure and separate.

In your dance together, find a way to soften and come together when you feel angry and apart. Find a way to let your armor dissolve as you look in silence into each other's eyes.

Your partner is not your enemy, although s/he sometimes seems to be. The separation you feel from one another is a function of your mutual fear. Come to each other as equals and admit your fear. Surrender your need to be right or to make your partner wrong. You are both right in your desire to be loved and respected by your partner. You are both wrong in your attempt to blame your partner for your unhappiness.

Come together as equals and say "Let us put this behind us...Let us begin again to see each other truly. Let us get in touch with our love and let go of our fear."

Relationship is a dance in a theater of wounds. As hard as you try to avoid hurting others, someone is always crying out in pain. Sometimes, an apology is necessary. But most of the time it is clear that one person's pain is triggered by someone else's. It's no one's fault. That's just the way it is.

After you have danced enough, you no longer take the drama so personally. You just get better at dancing out of your pain toward your joy. When you do that, the whole atmosphere on stage changes. An option arises that was not seen before.

To some, the earthly journey seems to be an arduous trek through a veil of tears. But even to these travelers, there are moments when the sun comes out and rainbows arch across the sky, moments when the pain slips away and the heart is filled with unexpected joy.

Even when the dance is difficult, one feels grateful for the opportunity to participate and to learn. Life is essentially dignified.

It is true that you resist and sometimes even refuse to learn your lessons. But learn them you do. You move onward and upward and, as you do, matter and mind become imbued with Spirit. Once identified with a specific mindset and a specific body, you will eventually be set free to love without conditions and to receive the love that is offered you without resisting or defending.

That is the nature of your journey here. It is a good journey. May you take the time to appreciate and enjoy it. May you open your eyes and see the sun peeking through the clouds. May you see the light reflected by the snow-covered ground and the white boughs of the pine trees. Light sparkling in all directions, embracing all of you, right here, right now.

Namaste

P aul Ferrini is the author of numerous books which help us heal the emotional body and embrace a spirituality grounded in the real challenges of daily life. Paul's work is heart-centered and experiential, empowering us to move through our fear and shame and share who we are authentically with others. Paul Ferrini founded and edited *Miracles Magazine*, a publication devoted to telling Miracle Stories offering hope and inspiration to all of us. Paul's conferences, retreats and *Affinity Group Process* have helped thousands of people deepen their practice of forgiveness and open their hearts to the Divine presence in themselves and others. For more information on Paul's workshops and retreats or *The Affinity Group Process*, contact Heartways Press, P.O. Box 181, South Deerfield, MA 01373 or call 413-665-0555.

Passionate Poems and a Love Story

Crossing The Water
Poems About Healing and
Forgiveness in Our Relationships by
Paul Ferrini

ISBN 1-879159-25-2
$9.95
96 pages, paperback

The time for healing and reconciliation has come, Ferrini writes. Our relationships help us heal childhood wounds, walk through our deepest fears, and cross over the water of our emotional pain. Just as the rocks in the river are *pounded and caressed to rounded stone,* the rough edges of our personalities are worn smooth in the context of a committed relationship. If we can keep our hearts open, we can heal together, experience genuine equality, and discover what it means to give and receive love without conditions.

Volume III of The Christ Mind Series is Hot Off the Press!

Miracle of Love, Reflections of the
Christ Mind, Part III by Paul Ferrini

ISBN 1-879159-23-6
$12.95, 192 pages, paperback

Many people say that this latest volume of the Christ Mind series is the best yet. Jesus tells us: "I was born to a simple woman in a barn. She was no more a virgin than your mother was." Moreover, he tells us, the virgin birth is not the only myth surrounding his life and teaching. So are the concepts of vicarious atonement and physical resurrection. Relentlessly, the master tears down the rigid dogma and hierarchical teachings that obscure his simple message of love and forgiveness. He encourages us to take him down from the pedestal and the cross and see him as an equal brother who found the way out of suffering by opening his heart totally. We too can open our hearts and find peace and happiness. "The power of love will make miracles in your life as wonderful as any attributed to me," he tells us. "Your birth into this embodiment is no less holy than mine. The love that you extend to others is no less important than the love I extend to you."

Now Finally our Bestselling Title on Audio Tape

Love Without Conditions, Reflections of the Christ Mind, Part I
by Paul Ferrini

The Book on Tape
Read by the Author
2 Cassettes,
Approximately 3.25 hours

ISBN 1-879159-24-4
$19.95

Now on audio tape: the incredible book from Jesus calling us to awaken to our own Christhood. Listen to this gentle, profound, book while driving in your car or before going to sleep at night. Elisabeth Kubler-Ross calls this "the most important book I have read. I study it like a Bible." Find out for yourself how this amazing book has helped thousands of people understand the radical teachings of the master and begin to integrate these teachings into their lives.

Heartways Press

"Integrating Spirituality into Daily Life"
More Books by Paul Ferrini

• Waking Up Together
Illuminations on the Road
to Nowhere

There comes a time for all of us when the outer destinations no longer satisfy and we finally understand that the love and happiness we seek cannot be found outside of us. It must be found in our own hearts, on the other side of our pain. "The Road to Nowhere is the path through your heart. It is not a journey of escape. It is a journey through your pain to end the pain of separation."

This book makes it clear that we can no longer rely on outer teachers or teachings to find our spiritual identity. Nor can we find who we are in relationships where boundaries are blurred and one person makes decisions for another. If we want to be authentic, we can't allow anyone else to be an authority for us, nor can we allow ourselves to be an authority for another person.

Authentic relationships happen between equal partners who take responsibility for their own consciousness and experience. When their buttons are pushed, they are willing to look at the obstacles they have erected to the experience of love and acceptance. As they understand and surrender the false ideas and emotional reactions that create separation, genuine intimacy becomes possible, and the sacred dimension of the relationship is born. 216 pp. paper ISBN 1-879159-17-1 $14.95

• The Ecstatic Moment:
A Practical Manual for Opening Your Heart and Staying in It.

A simple, power-packed guide that helps us take appropriate responsibility for our experience and establish healthy boundaries with others. Part II contains many helpful exercises and meditations that teach us to stay centered, clear and open in heart and mind. The Affinity Group Process and other group practices help us learn important listening and communication skills that can transform our troubled relationships. Once you have read this book, you will keep it in your briefcase or on your bedside table, referring to it often. You will not find a more practical, down to earth guide to contemporary spirituality. You will want to order copies for all your friends. 128 pp. paper ISBN 1-879159-18-X $10.95

• The Silence of the Heart
Reflections of the Christ Mind, Part Two

A powerful sequel to *Love Without Conditions*. John Bradshaw says: "with deep insight and sparkling clarity, this book demonstrates that the roots of all abuse are to be found in our own self-betrayal. Paul Ferrini leads us skillfully and courageously beyond shame, blame, and attachment to our wounds into the depths of self-forgiveness…a must read for all people who are ready to take responsibility for their own healing." 218 pp. paper. ISBN 1-879159-16-3 $14.95

• Love Without Conditions:
Reflections of the Christ Mind - Part I
An incredible book from Jesus calling us to awaken to our Christhood. Rarely has any book conveyed the teachings of the master in such a simple but profound manner. This book will help you to bring your understanding from the head to the heart so that you can model the teachings of love and forgiveness in your daily life. 192 pp. paper ISBN 1-879159-15-15 $12.00

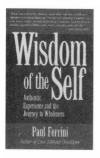

• The Wisdom of the Self
This ground-breaking book explores our authentic experience and our journey to wholeness. "Your life is your spiritual path. Don't be quick to abandon it for promises of bigger and better experiences. You are getting exactly the experiences you need to grow. If your growth seems too slow or uneventful for you, it is because you have not fully embraced the situations and relationships at hand...To know the Self is to allow everything, to embrace the totality of who we are, all that we think and feel, all of our fear, all of our love." 229 pp. paper ISBN 1-879159-14-7 $12.00

• The Twelve Steps of Forgiveness
A practical manual for healing ourselves and our relationships. This book gives us a step-by-step process for moving through our fears, projections, judgments, and guilt so that we can take responsibility for creating the life we want. With great gentleness, we learn to embrace our lessons and to find equality with others. A must read for all in recovery and others seeking spiritual wholeness. 128 pp. paper ISBN 1-879159-10-4 $10.00

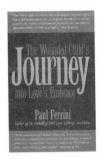

• The Wounded Child's Journey
Into Love's Embrace
This book explores a healing process in which we confront our deep-seated guilt and fear, bringing love and forgiveness to the wounded child within. By surrendering our judgments of self and others, we overcome feelings of separation and dismantle co-dependent patterns that restrict our self-expression and ability to give and receive love. 225pp. paper ISBN 1-879159-06-6 $12.00

• The Bridge to Reality
A Heart-Centered Approach to *A Course in Miracles* and the Process of Inner Healing. Sharing his experiences of spiritual awakening, Paul emphasizes self-acceptance and forgiveness as cornerstones of spiritual practice. Presented with beautiful photos, this book conveys the essence of *The Course* as it is lived in daily life. 192 pp. paper ISBN 1-879159-03-1 $12.00

• From Ego to Self
108 illustrated affirmations designed to offer you a new way of viewing conflict situations so that you can overcome negative thinking and bring more energy, faith and optimism into your life. 128 pp. paper ISBN 1-879159-01-5 $10.00

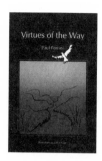

• Virtues of The Way
A lyrical work of contemporary scripture reminiscent of the Tao Te Ching. Beautifully illustrated, this inspirational book will help you cultivate the spiritual values required to fulfill your creative purpose and live in harmony with others. 64 pp. paper ISBN 1-879159-02-3 $7.50

• The Body of Truth
A crystal clear introduction to the universal teachings of love and forgiveness. This book traces all forms of suffering to negative attitudes and false beliefs, which we have the ability to transform. 64 pp. paper ISBN 1-879159-02-3 $7.50

• Available Light
Inspirational, passionate poems dealing with the work of inner integration, love and relationships, death and re-birth, loss and abundance, life purpose and the reality of spiritual vision. 128 pp. paper ISBN 1-879159-05-8 $12.00

Poetry and Guided Meditation Tapes
by Paul Ferrini

The Poetry of the Soul
With its heartfelt combination of sensuality and spirituality, Paul Ferrini's poetry has been compared to the poetry of Rumi. These luminous poems demonstrate why Paul Ferrini is first a poet, a lover and a mystic. Come to this feast of the beloved with an open heart and open ears. With Suzi Kesler on piano. $10.00 ISBN 1-879159-26-0

The Circle of Healing
The meditation and healing tape that many of you have been seeking. This gentle meditation opens the heart to love's presence and extends that love to all the beings in your experience. A powerful tape with inspirational piano accompaniment by Michael Gray. ISBN 1-879159-08-2 $10.00

Healing the Wounded Child
A potent healing tape that accesses old feelings of pain, fragmentation, self-judgment and separation and brings them into the light of conscious awareness and acceptance. Side two includes a hauntingly beautiful "inner child" reading from *The Bridge to Reality* with piano accompaniment by Michael Gray. ISBN 1-879159-11-2 $10.00

Forgiveness: Returning to the Original Blessing
A self healing tape that helps us accept and learn from the mistakes we have made in the past. By letting go of our judgments and ending our ego-based search for perfection, we can bring our darkness to the light, dissolving anger, guilt, and shame. Piano accompaniment by Michael Gray. ISBN 1-879159-12-0 $10.00

Paul Ferrini Talks and Workshop Tapes

Answering Our Own Call for Love *A Sermon given at the Pacific Church of Religious Science in San Diego, CA 11/97*

Paul tells the story of his own spiritual awakening, his Atheist upbringing, and how he began to open to the presence of God and his connection with Jesus and the Christ Mind teaching. In a very clear, heart-felt way, Paul presents to us the spiritual path of love, acceptance, and forgiveness. Also available on videotape. 1 Cassette *$10.00 ISBN 1-879159-33-3*

The Ecstatic Moment *A workshop given by Paul in Los Angeles at the Agape International Center of Truth, May, 1997*

Shows us how we can be with our pain compassionately and learn to nurture the light within ourselves, even when it appears that we are walking through darkness. Discusses subjects such as living in the present, acceptance, not fixing self or others, being with our discomfort and learning that we are lovable as we are. *1 Cassette $10.00 ISBN 1-879159-27-9*

Honoring Self and Other *A Workshop at the Pacific Church of Religious Science in San Diego, November, 1997*

Helps us understand the importance of not betraying ourselves in our relationships with others. Focuses on understanding healthy boundaries, setting limits, and saying no to others in a loving way. Real life examples include a woman who is married to a man who is chronically critical of her, and a gay man who wants to tell his judgmental parents that he has AIDS. *1 Cassette $10.00 ISBN 1-879159-34-1*

Seek First the Kingdom *Two Sunday Messages given by Paul: the first in May, 1997 in Los Angeles at the Agape Int'l. Center of Truth, and the second in September, 1997 in Portland, OR at the Unity Church.*

Discusses the words of Jesus in the Sermon on the Mount: "Seek first the kingdom and all else will be added to you." Helps us understand how we create the inner temple by learning to hold our judgments of self and other more compassionately. The love of God flows through our love and acceptance of ourselves. As we establish our connection to the divine within ourselves, we don't need to look outside of ourselves for love and acceptance. Includes fabulous music by The Agape Choir and Band. *1 Cassette $10.00 ISBN 1-879159-30-9*

Ending the Betrayal of the Self
A Workshop given by Paul at the Learning Annex in Toronto, April, 1997

A roadmap for integrating the opposing voices in our psyche so that we can experience our own wholeness. Delineates what our responsibility is and isn't in our relationships with others, and helps us learn to set clear, firm, but loving boundaries. Our relationships can become areas of sharing and fulfillment, rather than mutual invitations to co-dependency and self betrayal. *2 Cassettes $16.95 ISBN 1-879159-28-7*

Relationships: Changing Past Patterns *A Talk with Questions and Answers Given at the Redondo Beach Church of Religious Science, 11/97*

Begins with a Christ Mind talk describing the link between learning to love and accept ourselves and learning to love and accept others. Helps us understand how we are invested in the past and continue to replay our old relationship stories. Helps us get clear on what we want and understand how to be faithful to it. By being totally committed to ourselves, we give birth to the beloved within and also without. Includes an in-depth discussion about meditation, awareness, hearing our inner voice, and the Affinity Group Process. *2 Cassettes $16.95 ISBN 1-879159-32-5*

Relationship As a Spiritual Path *A workshop given by Paul in Los Angeles at the Agape Int'l. Center of Truth, May, 1997*

Explores concrete ways in which we can develop a relationship with ourselves and learn to take responsibility for our own experience, instead of blaming others for our perceived unworthiness. Also discussed: accepting our differences, the new paradigm of relationship, the myth of the perfect partner, telling our truth, compassion vs. rescuing, the unavailable partner, abandonment issues, negotiating needs, when to say no, when to stay and work on a relationship and when to leave. *2 Cassettes $16.95 ISBN 1-879159-29-5*

Opening to Christ Consciousness *A Talk with Questions & Answers at Unity Church, Tustin, CA November, 1997*

Begins with a Christ Mind talk giving us a clear picture of how the divine spark dwells within each of us and how we can open up to God-consciousness on a regular basis. Deals with letting go and forgiveness in our relationships with our parents, our children and our partners. A joyful, funny, and scintillating tape you will want to listen to many times. Also available on videotape. *2 Cassettes $16.95 ISBN 1-879159-31-7*

Risen Christ Posters and Notecards

11"x17" Poster
suitable for framing
ISBN 1-879159-19-8 $10.00

Set of 8 Notecards
with Envelopes
ISBN 1-879159-20-1 $10.00

Ecstatic Moment Posters and Notecards

8.5"x11" Poster
suitable for framing
ISBN 1-879159-21-X $5.00

Set of 8 Notecards
with Envelopes
ISBN 1-879159-22-8 $10.00

Heartways Press Order Form

Name_____

Address_____

City _____State _____Zip _____

Phone _____

BOOKS BY PAUL FERRINI

Return to the Garden ($12.95)   _____
Living in the Heart ($10.95)   _____
Miracle of Love ($12.95)   _____
Crossing the Water ($9.95)   _____
Waking Up Together ($14.95)   _____
The Ecstatic Moment ($10.95)   _____
The Silence of the Heart ($14.95)   _____
Love Without Conditions ($12.00)   _____
The Wisdom of the Self ($12.00)   _____
The Twelve Steps of Forgiveness ($10.00)   _____
The Circle of Atonement ($12.00)   _____
The Bridge to Reality ($12.00)   _____
From Ego to Self ($10.00)   _____
Virtues of the Way ($7.50)   _____
The Body of Truth ($7.50)   _____
Available Light ($10.00)   _____

AUDIO TAPES

The Circle of Healing ($10.00)   _____
Healing the Wounded Child ($10.00)   _____
Forgiveness: Returning to the Original Blessing ($10.00) _____
The Poetry of the Soul ($10.00)   _____
Seek First the Kingdom ($10.00)   _____
Answering Our Own Call for Love ($10.00)   _____
The Ecstatic Moment ($10.00)   _____
Honoring Self and Other ($10.00)   _____
Love Without Conditions ($19.95) 2 tapes   _____
Ending the Betrayal of the Self ($16.95) 2 tapes _____
Relationships: Changing Past Patterns ($16.95) 2 tapes _____
Relationship As a Spiritual Path ($16.95) 2 tapes _____
Opening to Christ Consciousness ($16.95) 2 tapes _____

Heartways Press Order Form

POSTERS AND NOTECARDS

Risen Christ Poster 11"x17" ($10.00) _____

Ecstatic Moment Poster 8.5"x11" ($5.00) _____

Risen Christ Notecards with envelopes 8/pkg ($10.00) _____

Ecstatic Moment Notecards with envelopes 8/pkg ($10.00) _____

SHIPPING

($2.00 for first item, $1.00 each additional item.
Add additional $1.00 for first class postage.) _____
MA residents please add 5% sales tax. _____

TOTAL $_____

Please allow 1-2 weeks for delivery

**Send Order To: Heartways Press
P. O. Box 181, South Deerfield, MA 01373
413-665-0555 • 413-665-0555
Toll free: 1-888-HARTWAY**

Coming in Early 1998

Return to the Garden
*Part IV of the Reflections of
The Christ Mind Series.*

Living in the Heart
*The Affinity Process and the Path of
Unconditional Love and Acceptance*

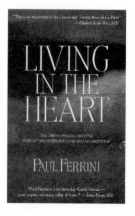